The Heart of It

A Series of Extracts from the Power of Silence

By Horatio W. Dresser

Published by Pantianos Classics

ISBN-13: 978-1-78987-064-0

First published in 1897

Contents

Preface.. *v*

Chapter One 8

God.. 8

Life 8

Mind and Matter 14

Evolution... 17

Growth 19

Experience... 22

Conduct... 25

Chapter Two... 29

Will.. 29

Desire... 30

Attention 31

Intuition.. 31

Tolerance 34

Belief 34

Chapter Three 35

Self 35

Asceticism.. 37

Fear... 38

Doubt 39

Evil 40

Chapter Four.. 41

Personality 41

Individuality 42

Atmospheres 43

Fate 44

Happiness 47

Beauty 47

Chapter Five **48**

Silence 48

Healing 49

Mastery 53

Revelation 54

The Whole 55

Preface

Under ordinary circumstances, two books whose existence is a matter of only a year or so would hardly call for an anthology, — a compression of the meat of both into smaller limits. Yet the request for such compression has become a demand. The readers of the two volumes, "The Power of Silence" and "The Perfect Whole," while they will in no ways renounce the ownership of the substantial volumes, want a digest, — something that may slip into the pocket, be the companion of a railway journey, a bedside book; in short, one of the "little books" easy to handle and the synonym for tonic, strengthener, upbuilder.

To make such compilation and arrange the extracts under the headings — the grouping of which, as will be seen, follows the logical and philosophical order of development — has been a labor of love. It has also served to deepen and fix the impression made in the early reading of the two volumes, repeated afterward with deliberate intention to criticize at every point. As eager seekers of light on the "new thought," countless disappointments had been met. While the spirit and intention of many books and pamphlets was admirable, there was for the most a fatal lack of fine literary quality, of any background of real knowledge, any large outlook on life as a whole.

Naturally, then, the books were approached critically. A profound student of religions, philosophies, and life, a worker of the noblest order, with an insight and a critical quality that are always unfailing tests of the value of book or word, Mrs. Westendorf's final judgment of the book meant to my own mind more than a thousand average reviewers could effect. Read three times, every salient point, every choice passage, was marked; and it is these markings that form the present volume.

The verdict on the work was a singularly impartial one. "The Power of Silence" came to us with no knowledge of either its author or its background, was judged solely on its own merits, and pronounced for the "new thought" an epoch-making book. None of the ordinary methods appear to have been used with it, its author having small relish for any of them, and believing that, if it were worth place, place would be made for it.

Unheralded, then, by any announcements, making its way by sheer force of the quality of the work it held, "The Power of Silence" has already, at present writing [Jan. I, 1897], passed into its fifth edition; while its successor, "The Perfect Whole," is having much the same experience. The opening chapter of "The Power of Silence," "The Immanent God," appeared first in pamphlet form, and the steady demand for it compelled the printing of a large edition; while another chapter, "The Meaning of Suffering," has also taken this shape, and is now widely known.

The present compilers planned for their work before the fact was known that any direct call had been made for it. With full knowledge of admirable work already in the field, and destined at every turn to meet varying needs as help and guide, — Henry Wood, notably. Miss Ellen Dyer, Dr. Emily Cady, Lilian Whiting, standing for some of the best presentation of the thought, — Mr. Dresser's books are a step beyond, the thorough philosophical training of the author giving him an authority not to be lightly questioned, while his power of expression illumines the closest argument. The spirit and the power of Emerson are both there, but there is something more. It is Emerson humanized, as it were, — brought into more vital relation with the needs, small and great, of daily life. With this faith in the work, this conviction that its mission has but begun, and the certainty that in these closing most pregnant years of the nineteenth century its influence is to be felt at every step in our forward march toward the dawning day for all, the compilers end their
work, and give it God-speed.

Helen Campbell
Cincinnati, Ohio
January 1, 1897.

"Oh, balanced like a whirling star,
The all-untiring forces are,
Enveloped in their vast career.
With their own silent atmosphere,—
A Faith that, in its calmness great.
Shows the self-consciousness of Fate,
And that unconquerable Will
Which, mastering all, is swift and still.
"Ah, then, possess thy soul in peace,
Thou Builder for the centuries!
Since all our mightiest forces run.
Still and resistless as the sun."
"Die milde Macht 1st gross."

— **Goethe**

Chapter One

God

God is our larger, our diviner self, nearer to us than thought, closer than thought can imagine. His relation to us must ever be intimate, since there is no power, no substance, no space, to separate us. Therefore we are not, in any sense, apart from him. We exist with him in a relationship typified by that of a child in its mother's arms. He is our Father, though infinite in power and wisdom. Nothing can prevent us from enjoying his love, his help, his peace, his inspiring guidance, but our own failure to recognize his presence. Let us, then, be still, and know his love, his indwelling presence. Let us test it fully, and learn what it will do for us if we never worry, never fear, never reach out and away from this present life. Let us absorb from his love, as the plant absorbs from the sunlight; for our spirits, like the plants, need daily nourishment.

If gravitation holds the earth in its position in space, may it not be that its spiritual counterpart, the love of God, sustains our souls in their progress, and
provides for us in ways which we have scarcely suspected? Yet how many of thosewho say, "God is love," stop to realize the world of meaning in that little sentence? There is healing and comfort in such realization.

Life

The one great essential in human life is to become deeply conscious of this eternal relationship, to learn its individual meaning, to co-operate with the uplifting spirit within, to attain peace, equanimity, and health through willing service and obedience, through comprehensive thinking and many-sided development.

Mere human wit seems incompetent to make much headway in the great search for the heart of life. One waits for some golden moment when life may, perchance, reveal its secret in passing, and put an end to this petty in-quiry into the great mysteries of thought. There are, indeed, times when a sublime and unmistakable conviction is present in consciousness, bearing its own evidence with it. It is these hidden touches of truth in our poor descrip-tions of life which give them their only permanent value. Out of these secret pencillings of the higher self one can, in time, formulate a general scheme of the meaning of things, trusting to the instinct of the reader to restore the original setting, shorn of the crude details which inevitably encumber all our attempts to reproduce the real.

Quicken a man's interest in so-called spiritual things, and you shall find him neglecting his body and the interests of his physical life. A mistaken philosophy, reappearing in new forms, has for ages sanctioned this neglect; and a current phase of the doctrine assures us that we should avoid giving attention to externals. Other people are starving their spiritual natures by excessive devotion to lifeless dogmas and the enticing pleasures of social and intellectual life. Everywhere one finds a want of balance between theory and practice, mind and body, culture and the spirit, the demands of self and the needs of others; between the receiving, accumulating, and developing of property and ideas and the just distribution of that which is rightfully ours only that we may share it Fragments of men one may find, — good theorists, laborers, and servants. But how far one must search for the well-rounded character, equally sound in mind and body, whose life spontaneously and easily maintains its equilibrium with that balance of spirit and form typified by those rare musicians in whom melody and technique are so combined that they sing or play in perfect tune!

For to those who have clearly grasped this intimately close relationship of divine shareholding and service of the whole by each and of the whole for each, there is just one righteous course open for all future conduct; namely, to follow an ethical life, a life of strict honesty, justice, sincerity, enthusiasm for the right, the true, and the good, and of devotion to a high ideal.

No one worthy of the name of man — that is, one whose privilege it is to overcome and to obey — can in fact see the full significance of the ethical ideal who does not straightway begin to make his life conform to it. Heretofore one may have intended to do right, but failed or unconsciously obeyed a general impulse toward the good. But now one becomes an intelligent moral agent through actual knowledge of the unity of life, the singleness of the moral goal, and the duty which each one is called upon to play in a world where to live is to share and to serve.

The ideal state of society is rather one in which each man stands for what he is worth, where each receives a fair proportion of what he earns, where no one holds a monopoly of power or wealth, nor any authority which takes away the freedom or the natural rights of man, since the earth belongs to men, not to man, and since no one may create a monopoly nor oppress the sexes, morally or industrially, without committing a sin in the name of the highest and divinest law.

One might live a thousand years in the presence of all this peace and wisdom, yet be wholly unconscious of it as long as allegiance to person, creed, dogma, and the cares and pleasures of our surface life, hold unquestioned sway; and, although the road to the higher life and equanimity again and again opens up before the mind, never until the last connection is broken with the lower interests, when one really cares more for the Spirit than for all its passing forms, does one at last fully enter this changeless realm of the eternal.

That which my soul attracts is what I need, that of which I am most deeply convinced will reveal to me the secret of the universe; and, as long as I harmonize my conduct with this deepest attraction, I may rest assured that I am leading a wisely spiritual life. Life may seem far more complex than this. This simple rule may seem incapable of universal application. But here, at any rate, is the ideal, the key to life's mystery; namely, its purest spirit or love, that which holds all elsein intelligible solution.

The fact that we cannot seize the soul in the act of self-expression is by no means a proof that it is not there; for we only know it through its manifestations, and through the discovery that it persistently means the same ideal Moreover, during illness it is not this inmost part of us that is sick, nor is it affected by evil and wrong-doing. It is rather an imprisoned spectator of all this, longing to master the conditions of sense, but not quite free. It does not grow old with its body. It feels itself not only superior to space and time, but even now capable of living under conditions other than those of matter.

Oh, how one longs to express the glory and beauty of life from this higher point of view, how one longs for some stronger language, or for some means of communicating to the untold thousands to whom life is still a mystery and a burden that fundamentally, and for them, when they shall be quickened to see it, life is really a joy, an apocalypse crystal clear, through which appears the fair spirit of transcendent Being ! Here, within, one shall be forever refreshed at will. Little by little the outer world will appear more beautiful, and one's burden less heavy. All truth, all power, all wisdom and love, are here in this one limitless present eternity. Every moment repeats the beauty of the whole. Every fact of our sense life is related to it. The Spirit that possesses itself in this eternity knows us, loves us, needs us, — you and me. There is no other power, no other reality, no other perfect friend.

No gift is worth the sacrifice of equanimity and calm self-possession. One is inclined to express such visions in paeans of ecstasy, like the psalms of old. But no, it bids one be poised and moderate. Not in bursts of enthusiastic praise shall the deepest emotions be expressed, nor in one-sided development, as though the spiritual insight were all-sufficient. It is good only through its results. If one becomes open to it little by little, expanding with its life, growing pure in the presence of its love, it will gradually and harmoniously transform the whole being, overcome and transmute all that is not brought into subjection, and lift the finite life to the exalted plane of wise obedience to the perfect will of the infinite.

As high as one ascends, the Spirit is therefore still the beyond, the life of all that moves in every part of the Perfect Whole. Instead of wandering off into the leveling visions of mysticism, one's attitude thus fortunately becomes one of humility and worship, since he who claims to know all and to be all is thereby cut off from true wisdom. One has ascended to this higher plane to learn, to be purified and freed from the constraints of sense. One should therefore open one's self to receive, to be guided and strengthened, that one may once more take up the roundof temporal life, and carry the spirit there. Rest and silence are preparatory to labor and thought. One should therefore cultivate the silence rather as the highest in a long series of experiences than as anything final in itself. Only in this way can one avoid developing too rapidly in the spiritual life.

One awaits these moments, not merely as the oases of life, — for existence is never wearisome to those who know them, — but as moments when so much is added to one's self that all else seems like mere filling, the mere development of that which here resides in inexhaustible essence. At other times one can half persuade one's self to doubt and to look at life's darker side as though it had no compensation. But, when these insights come, the whole wide universe of beings and things is seen to be of one piece in the great life of God, whose infinite beauty, love, and goodness receive their full manifestation in that unsearchable whole whose name is eternity.

Eternity is the setting of the moment as truly as of the century, and it is ever herewhere time is in deepest truth no more, ever there where space is a mere detail in the boundless picture of the Ineffable. A new life, a new world, opens like a vista before the mind when one thus turns aside from the hurry and care of daily life with the calm realization that in this present moment one is a living soul dwelling in the boundless realm of the eternal now.

It is acceptance of life, not as the changing circumstances of the moment present it, — for all that now is is to give way to a better condition, — but adjustment to life as a whole, as it shall be, as it is eternally. It is not the contentment of satisfaction, of settled conviction and conservatism, of selfishness and comfort. It is contentment through knowledge of growth, through the conviction that one is of service to the world, and the readiness to exchange a poor doctrine for a better.

In order to gain this poise, then, one must really desire it, and consciously seek the inner stillness. There, in that quiet inner center, in the living, present Reality, in whose love and wisdom one may repose in peaceful trust, — there is to be found the beneficent essence so long obscured by the false theology and thoughtless belief of the past It exists, it abounds, it abides. There is no need to consult books or persons, no need to approach it through the media of petitions and ceremonies. One simply needs to discover that the very life by which we exist is a part of this abiding presence persisting through all the mutations of time, and then to rise to a plane superior to the sensations, the self-interests, fears, beliefs, and pleasures which have so long held us in bondage to matter. For self-scrutiny shows that there is a part of us which endures, despite all change in the outer man.

In such a realization as this, that we blend in consciousness and in love with the ever-renewing Life, and that we reveal more and more of the divine nature as we ascend in the scale of being, lies a real way of escape from morbid self-interest, introspection, self-consciousness, want of confidence, and the feeling of one's own insignificance. To know that our highest love, our deepest thought, our truest self, is not wholly our own, but, in so far as it is unselfish, is divine, — this it is to have something in which we can trust and on which we can rely, which shows us what we are, not as weak human beings which we vainly try to understand by self-analysis, but what we are as particles of the divine nature.

We are expressions of the infinite life, yet are finite just because the all-seeing intelligence means one thing in your life, and something else in mine. We are imperfect, incomplete, because we join with others to form his meaning; and he hasnot yet reflected our lives to their perfect conclusion, — a process which we are confident he will complete, though it take eternity.

Unless our activity is due ultimately to the one life, then there is an existence independent of it; and this we have proved impossible. Our consciousness, our life, our intelligence, must blend with the infinite life and consciousness; and this larger life must. therefore, be all of, yet more than our own. Since this Reality is omnipresent, and is the sum total of all that exists, we must be part of it in order to exist at all, and as dependent on it as the plant on the sunlight. And, since it must be conscious in order to be aware of its own existence, it must know us as a part of itself.

The great secret of life is to know how, in our own way, to be receptive to it, how to read the message of its inner whispering. The sure method of growing strong in realization of its nearness is to believe it will come if we listen, to trust it in moments of doubt as the lost hunter trusts his horse in the forest, to have an ideal outlook, and then renew our realization, day by day, ever remembering that, as this Spirit is the only Reality, the one power, the one love, we live in it, and with it, and there is naught to separate us from its ever-watchful care, its ever-loving presence.

Life, then, all life, yours and mine, all that holds it together and links it with the eternal forces of the universe, is a continuous, divine communication. There is no separation between our own souls and that Spirit in whom, in the most literal sense, we live and move and have our being, between the world in which we live and that eternal Reality of whose substance and of whose activity it is a part. The life which sleeps in the rock, dreams in the plant, and awakens to consciousness in man, is the same, the one great life, which is revealed just as clearly in the fortuitous changes that spur us on to progress as in the exact movements of the planets.

We are absorbed in the present, in its needs and woes, unaware that our whole past lives, our inheritance and our temperament, may affect this bit of suffering nature which, for the moment, limits our thought. Thus experience everywhere lacks perspective. Our thinking is painfully narrow. We do not look far enough. We live as though time were soon to cease, and prudence would not permit us an hour for quiet reflection.

Yet a new phase, and to some the happiest phase, of life begins when we become conscious of our intimate relation to eternity, when we stop hurried thought, and try quietly to realize what life means as a progressing whole. If life be one, and reveal one purpose, one God, can any other interpretation be rational, will the parts ever assume their true relationship in our minds except when viewed in the light of the whole?

There is no time for complaint, or even for suffering, so far as suffering is self-caused, if we dwell in this pure region of thought, where we look upon the good and true as an outburst of the divine, and all else as slowly evolving toward this realm of goodness, where the landscape suggests the beauty which it so well typifies, and where our own hardships lead us, not into the realm of complaint, but into the land of inquiry, of genuine desire to know what God is doing with us.

There is a new demand made upon man, — to understand himself in the light of all the causes that have operated to produce him, his thought, his daily experience, his joy and suffering. Man cannot fully understand himself without constant reference to the omnipresent Spirit in whom he lives, and in this profoundest wisdom is to be found the one unfailing resource in every moment of need.

Do we let this life come as it may from the divine source, without rebellion, without doubt, carrying before us an ever-renewed ideal of ourselves as happy, useful, in good health, every day in our experience having some meaning in the divine economy? Do we turn from matter to the Reality behind it; from the body to the soul that molds it, now in this fashion, now in that, by the power of thought; from the ills which seem so real while we dwell upon them to the inner self which can become so strong that we shall have no ills whatever except those which are essential to our truest evolution?

Yet, if this world-order is the best possible order, the love of God must be just as clearly manifested in the struggles which carry us along until we think as in our moments of repose. It is character that avails, that seems to be the purpose of our contests; and character is the result of determined effort to surmount the obstacles we are compelled to meet until we learn to live above our troubles. The experiences, of evil and suffering seem justified by their outcome, since we should know nothing without experience.

The utmost that one individual can do for another is to enunciate the principles which underlie all experiences, however varied. Truth is not truth for us until we have made it our own through reflection, until we have applied it in daily life.

Life is a constant readjustment. It requires a daily renewal of one's faith, and then a return to the tasks, the struggles, which at times well-nigh weigh us down. It means repeated failure. It means a thorough test of all that is in us. It often means trouble and discouragement, whenever one gets new light and regenerative ideas, since a period of darkness similar to the decay of the seed in the ground follows every incoming of greater power. But it is priceless knowledge to know that we are equal to the occasion. It is a long step toward self-understanding when we learn to see in facts that once caused discouragement profound reasons for hope and cheer. It is a decided step toward self-mastery when we learn to meet these ups and downs, these regenerative periods, in a broadly philosophical spirit, at once superior to our circumstances and to the thoughts and fears

which once held us in their power. It is fortunate, indeed, if we no longer deem life's task too hard, if our faith be sufficiently strong to sustain us through the severest tests, thereby proving our fitness to be made better, our willingness to persist, though all be dark, with an iron determination to succeed.

Have we really begun to live, are we even half what we should be, whiffed about as we are by opinions and fears, at the mercy of other minds and of our own unconquered selves? Half the facts of life go to show that man is a product of matter, and his thoughts and feelings mere effects of a fateful outer cause. The other half show that he is a master, — a master in embryo, it may be, but a sharer of the only Life and the only Power by virtue of his individual will and his invincible power of thought. Life and all it brings him, ultimately, depends on his own wisdom and the intelligence he puts into it. He is weak and fearful, at the mercy of matter and passion, only as long as he lacks understanding. To know self and overcome it, to know the law and obey it, — this is the sum of righteousness; and all that duty demands of us at first is to make the start, to remember nature's law of growth, and persistency to keep the great end in view.

Mind and Matter

Contrast is fundamental to consciousness; and without it our inner experience would be like an external world of one color, or a world where only the roar of Niagara should prevail. Without mind we could not know matter, and without changes of energy or contrast we should not possess mind. Extreme idealists, on the one hand, and short-sighted materialists, on the other, theoretically annihilate the entire universe and themselves by denying the existence of either mind or matter. The attempt to derive mind from matter is no less a failure. The two have evolved together, and are so many general instances of the two-sided experience which, beginning in infancy, extends through life.

It is only by relation with other minds and an unyielding outer world that we learn of our existence at all. Without the cooperation of other minds, without language, social fellowship, and experience of natural phenomena, we should be unable to organize and understand our conscious experience: we should have no conscious experience. This fact has great significance for the ethical life.

If the mystic in his unwordable transport could at last really throw aside the veil of sense, of finite life and the natural world, and behold the eternal oneness, recognizing himself so that all illusion should vanish, then for him all earthly communication would cease, there would be no earth and no unregenerate with whom to communicate. For the moment he "descends to meet," and attempts to clothe his vision in the homely garb of finite speech, he indubitably admits the existence of the world which he hopes to convert and the language whereby he contradicts his own doctrine. In fact, it is characteristic of all who insist that mind or the immediate is the all of being to show by their conduct that they believe most heartily in the existence of both matter and evil; while some of the advocates of irrational idealism are most strenuous in their endeavor for this world's goods.

We suffer pain and observe the effects of evil, we perceive and handle matter; and, if it be not as substantial as it seems, it at least exists as an appearance for which our wills are not responsible. It is surely no explanation of error, evil, and matter to say that they do not exist. To call these facts illusion, and then not to account for them, is merely a shifting of terms. The facts are still with us, awaiting interpretation. It is the discovery of just what illusion or error is that we desire most deeply to make. We cannot be utterly deceived in thus representing a world; and, if we are simply dreaming, then by all means let us have a consistent theory of dreams.

We may, then, call the world by any term we choose, so long as we really understand what we mean, so long as we make two important discriminations between (1) the world as it exists for the infinite Self, its sufficient ground or reality, who knows it absolutely as it is, (2) and the world as it exists for finite beings in general, the realm of uniformity and order, of scientific observation, — the world as any particular finite being may perceive it, colored by the kind or grade of intelligence.

Every manifestation, every formative force, becomes instinct with Life; and in observing the minutest microscopic detail we are discovering the wonderful discrimination, the unwordably beautiful diversification of the divine mind thus Systematically revealed. To spurn one fact is to despise its divine origin. To confuse the two sides of being is to surrender all intelligibility. To mistake the two for a duality, in any sense separable, is to be ignorant of the sublimest truth of life; namely, that the one is the description or consciousness of the other, viewed now as whole, now as constituent parts, now as living essence, and now as awareness that it lives.

Although that which is for me "gravitates to me," I have to become ready for it. I must do my part. In a word, my efforts are successful in proportion as I imitate nature, and work both objectively and subjectively. I thus avoid the extremes of materialism, on the one hand, and of self-centered subjectivism,

15

on the other. To a certain degree I must change both myself and the world, so far as bodily and Social imperfections are concerned. I may then see the world beautiful; that is, so far as I am a living embodiment of the absolute and eternal Beauty of the universe, in so far as I stand for a beautiful fact. Whether my world of beauty is the same as yours, I could never definitely know unless I could view both my life and yours from the standpoint of the Absolute. Thus far I am explicitly finite. My beauty, in relation to the divine economy, consists in my limitations. It would be a serious mistake for me to say that I, as a finite being, can behold the world from the absolute point of view. It would be equally erroneous to say that my own ignorance is the basis of this wonderfully beautiful arrangement.

As finite beings, we are not all of God, we are organs of the divine nature,
—
many believe that we shall never be wholly absorbed, — and to efface all distinctions is to surrender the very consciousness or character whereby we are made to stand for some fact in the great self-manifestation of the perfect All. The finite, since it exists, is essential to the perfection of the infinite. A whole without parts is a massively exclusive monotony, an utter nonentity. A God without consciousness, manifestation, and an experience full of contrasts and distinctions, is a bare nothing; but a whole with parts, a God with self-cognition, and beings whom he can love and through whom he can reveal himself, is just such a reality made known through the beautiful world of finite selves, of law and order, qualities and relations, as we now happily possess.

Sympathetic discrimination is the guide to truth, and probably there is no surer way to avoid inconsistency than fearlessly and patiently to reduce all our beliefs to their logical simplicity. If our statements imply, as in the case of mysticism, that reality is rationally unknowable, then we may know that we have somewhere gone astray. And not until we are ready to lay aside every theory we may have held in the past, whenever a better doctrine is presented, do we really care more for truth than for the forms and personalities in which it is clothed.

A very subtle form of self-conceit has grown up among students of occult science and Hindu lore, as though the intellect only existed as a fit object for their scorn, Western science as a synonym for ignorance, and their own dogmas as other forms of eternal truth. Such people have wandered far from the true spirit. No one needs intellectual cultivation so much as those who thus decry it. Only he, let me repeat, whose doctrine is visionary, unsubstantial, and inconsistent, he who has neglected to ask himself precisely what he means by the terms he uses, by his belief and his faith, thereby endeavoring to eliminate all mysticism, would ever think of decrying human reason, the one balance wheel of all our thinking.

The relation of God to matter is therefore just as intimate as his relation to the human soul, for whatever exists is a part of and within the one Reality.

We cannot, then, consistently deny the existence of matter. To make such a denial is equivalent to asserting the non-existence of the one Reality, and therefore of our sensations, since all that we experience has some cause outside ourselves; and we know our own existence only as it is related to this outer Reality. Matter surely exists. Mind exists. How they are related in consciousness we shall soon consider. But we must begin with matter as a real existence, as a part of God, imbued with his immanent life, and in no sense independent of him. The one Reality must be the basis and substance, and the only basis and substance, of all that we call matter, just as truly as it is the Life that is active in every moment and in every incident of our inmost being.

Matter, then, is not a mere phenomenon, any more than is the mind that partially knows it. Ultimately, it is a real substance. It is part of the one enduring Reality, the cause or series of causes of the world of sense-experience. It is the real substance partially perceived and judged according to our opinions and temperament: it is the means whereby we contemplate the One. Reality is both the universe as God knows it and the God who knows it. As matter, it is his meaning, his purpose made manifest: it is God realizing himself in definite form, the tangible expression of his purpose holding man in the straight and narrow pathway of progress, the Spirit put in limited form so that we can grasp it.

But nature is not only a law-governed unit, a mechanism animated by a single force, in which the varying substances are Composed of minute particles. It is also a live organism, in which each part, each organ, pulsating with energy and instinct with life, has some meaning as related to the whole. Of this great unitary organism, throbbing with life from star to atom, man is an integrant part. He is related to it so closely that he seems, in fact, the central figure, whose life was prophesied from the very dawn of being. History, religion, science, literature, present this relationship in a thousand different lights; and now a new science of sociology and ethics is taking shape in men's minds, showing that society is also an organism in which each man owes some duty to his human brotherhood.

Matter seems like a mere Symbol as compared with this its real meaning. The Life which manifested itself so long ago in the primeval history of the earth returns to consciousness in man, and recognizes through him its own transcendent source. The soul knows the great unity henceforth, whatever be the phase of it contemplated. It habitually turns from the universe to God, and from God to his great world of manifestation.

Evolution

To many evolution simply means the derivation of man from some lost ancestor, a belief which generally arouses a feeling of repugnance; or it means that the existence of God is not necessary under this theory, and one naturally lays it aside as irreligious. Yet evolution would be of little value if it were not a universal law, just as well exemplified in the growth of the tree as in the development of new species or of a planet from a mass of nebula. It would have no ultimate meaning unless it proved the presence of God at every step in the great world process.

We have an excellent example of what evolution means in the growth of our own ideas. We are born with a certain set of opinions on matters of religion, politics, and the like. There is a strong tendency toward conservatism; and we are inclined to think like our parents, and even to cherish and defend the dogmas which have come down to us. But with each experience, each new book, each new acquaintance with the world and with people, which makes an impression on us, a new factor enters into our thought; and the only way to avoid progress is to avoid contact with progressive people.

Our own deepest self challenges us to find any possible method of growth and change except that of patient evolution, the great world-wide process of "continuous progressive change, according to unvarying laws, and by means of resident forces." The process once called creation is as long as time itself, as wide as the universe. It is going on today. It will never cease until its great task be completed. It is thorough, painstaking, gradual, and sure. It is economical, careful, and direct, making use of every incident, every possible factor, every so-called chance, so that in human life joy, sorrow, hardship, success, heredity, disposition, environment, education, society, and thought are called into use; and all these factors have their meaning, their bearing on the ideal result. "The ideal is immanent in the real." The aspiring force speaks through the slightest incident of experience. The all-powerful, omnipresent Spirit aspires through, co-operates with, and seeks cooperation from the individual soul to whom it is ever trying to make itself known. God is immanent in evolution.

Man is a progressive being. He is not yet completed; and the law of his growth is evolution. He may hinder that growth in a thousand different ways; and much depends on his attitude toward it, as we shall see in the next chapter. But he only changes the world as it appears to him, not as it exists in reality. Co-operation with it, with evolution, is his one greatest lesson. To learn how to adjust himself to the organism of which he forms a part is his great task; and the law of aspiration by which all evolution is guided is the direction of mind which is for him the one essential. His follies and fears will die of inanition. His harmful states of mind will cease to trouble him if he refuse them the attention which is their life. The source of the mental organism, in which he is a factor, is just as truly the immanent Life as the outer order of nature. It has a certain tendency, which he can follow if he will; and, if he follow it consciously and reflectively, his thought will constantly lead him back to the great Originator, in whom the worlds of nature and of our mental life are one.

Growth

Nothing leaps into being. A plant cannot blossom until it has reached the proper stage. My success in any undertaking is commensurate with the energy I put forth. If I meet a man whose presence is wonderfully stimulating, it is because we have something in common, and because my past experience, my desires, and thought have prepared me for this new development. In order to know a thing, I "must have a share of its nature in myself." All our relations with the world depend on ourselves and on what the world is. For everything that we see without, there is some corresponding mental state within; and whether we are happy or miserable, successful or unsuccessful, wise or ignorant, depends more upon our mental attitude than upon the most fixed and fateful conditions of nature. Fate, evil, and suffering, as we shall see, are in fact so many unyielding obstacles or are plastic and comprehensible, according as we view them.

The narrow, rut-bounded religious believer knows not that he is narrow until a happy chance brings him to self-consciousness. Perhaps the chief benefit of foreign travel is the opportunity of viewing ourselves and our neighbors from a distance. We progress when we are disturbed, when our easy-going conservatism and self-satisfaction are upset by new ideas. Until we meet our superiors, we are apt to take credit to ourselves for wisdom and spirituality. But a day comes when all that we have said and done seems mean and insignificant in comparison with the glorious possibilities ideally presented to view.

The half-developed animal man who commits one crime and is then condemned to a life among those upon whom a thoughtless society has set its stamp as incurably "depraved" instead of treating them as human beings to be elevated, may not be nearly as wicked as the cruel capitalist who oppresses his employees as though they were slaves, or those who throughout their lives make it easy for the sinner whom society accepts as of good repute. We all dwell together in human society, and necessarily partake of its ills and its blessings. He who condemns is not himself above guilt. He who seems good and virtuous is often deemed such because our standards are so low and partial.

There is a growing tendency to look upon the evil-minded man as the unbalancedman, the one who misdirects his forces, he who is not yet truly a man. Evil, then, is not in any sense an entity: it is slavery; and he who is enslaved needs to be enlightened, to be made aware of higher standards, and taught to see the real economy of obedience to them. We thus avoid the difficulty of attributing evil directly to God, since evil, as we know it and are enslaved by it, is primarily human. With God it is more probably viewed as means to an end, and therefore understood in the light of its outcome.

One has gained power and self-development because circumstances have called out the best that lay dormant within, not because one knew in advance how to win truth and virtue. For all who have really attained self-possession and poise, experience has been such as to test human faith to the utmost, as though Nature were determined to defeat us if she could. Yet we have survived, and our contests were not nearly as critical as we feared at the time.

The lower nature, like fate or law, is a blessing or a curse, according to our use of it. Nothing could be more beautiful than the law which compels us to suffer until we come to judgment, and then frees us from suffering because we have learned the necessity and place of the two sides of our nature. Evil and suffering are only necessary, then, up to a certain point. After that they do not exist, for us, since everything, when understood, is seen to be a means to an end, and therefore good. To understand life so that all friction shall cease, and every act be turned to good account, is, in a word, the ideal of all our progress.

Once more, it is casting aspersions upon the wisdom and love of God, if he be not competent to "redeem" the wickedest of his creatures. And, if he can redeem them all, it is no argument against the beauty of the universe that such sinners exist For just how he can redeem any particular sinner only he in his perfect wisdom could know. It is enough for us if we understand the principle, and see how in our own lives every error is a partial truth, and every sin so far good as it serves a purpose.

It is argued by some that God could not know our mistakes nor suffer with us. But how, then, could he perfect us, how could he be Absolute, unless he knew both the temptation and the victory through heroic achievement by which it is finally overcome? Is he not himself immanent in our moral contests, himself the higher power by which we master the lower?

If the experience of self-consciousness shows that we have hitherto lived wholly for self, the compensation is already apparent in so far as reflection has now taught us to understand and obey the higher law; and, surely, our disobedience of the moral law was not mere sinfulness, if it taught us the imperative nature of that law. And the next step is to adjust one's self to the higher and lower forces, so that they shall work together for good.

Never work with mere effects, do not dwell upon the process nor look at obstacles and conditions, — by themselves, — but face toward the light, look at the outcome, take the college settlement into the slums, take the higher to the lower, remembering that the mere presence of the higher is sufficient to create new standards.

Remember that most of our suffering, and the larger part of our endeavor to overcome it, are unnecessary. All existence is an aim, all desire indicates the presence of the Higher with us; and our part is to let the Spirit have its way through us, to let it work like leaven till all the life is transfigured from within, from lower to higher, from higher to still higher, until the Christ-spirit shall prevail.

It is clear that every describable experience has a positive basis; and, whatever we call a state where darkness predominates, it is never without a definite cause. A negation as applied to the manifestations of reality, in fact, explains nothing. When the sun sets, we experience a change, and govern ourselves accordingly; for we have learned to know darkness through comparison with light. The fiendish scheming of the criminal is undeniably positive; and, if there is any experience in the world that is emphatically the presence of something, it is physical suffering, and the crying evils of our boasted civilization. Such tendencies are surely not the mere privation of good, nor are they merely "good in the making." They are the centrifugal forces of our progress, without which progress could not be. The lower is just as good, just as necessary as the higher — in its place. Both would seem good and beautiful, could we view them as they really are in the light of the whole.

If a man really sees the beauty of righteousness and desires to practice the moral law, this is of itself sufficient to cause regeneration; and he will begin almost unconsciously to realize his ideal. Meanwhile he may sometimes unnecessarily condemn himself as a hypocrite when he is, in truth, progressing as rapidly as his own obstinate lower nature will permit.

But, when a man at last sees the imperative nature of the moral law, understands a rational or ethical precept, and is thereby convinced of its soundness, its beauty, and its universality; when conscience assures him of the right, — if he does not then obey it, he is guilty of renouncing the most sacred obligation of the universe, and of deliberately turning aside from the pathway of righteousness and truth to follow his own lowest self, thereby virtually denying the genuineness of truth, disbelieving his own reason, and surrendering his right to be called a sincere, upright, moral man.

One should act from reason, not from impulse, even when it is a question of self-denial or of immediate good, and make self-realization not a personal, but a social end, so that every detail of life may be transfigured with the sense of its moral worth. If self-consciousness shows me that I am weak, one-sided, the cause of my own. misery and unhappiness, it is for me to overcome all this by getting out of self, by gaining my balance through service to humanity.

Whenever one asks these great questions, — whether to do the present good and sacrifice the possible future good, giving up self-development it may be, or to look far ahead and adjust means to the ultimate end, one is bringing together the two elements which in one form or another constitute every fact of life. The scholar, devoted to some great scientific pursuit, may be deemed exceedingly selfish by those who demand all sorts of present deeds of philanthropy from him; while, in truth, the genuine scholar denies himself half the pleasures of life, in order to serve the truth. It is unquestionably wrong for one who really possesses ability of a high order to dedicate his life to the passing deeds of the moment, when he might the better serve humanity by devoting himself to his special talent.

All truth, all power, all wisdom and love, are here in this one limitless pre sent eternity. Every moment repeats the beauty of the whole. Every fact of our sense-life is related to it. The Spirit that possesses itself in this eternity knows us, loves us, needs us, — you and me. There is no other power, no other reality, no other perfect friend. Nothing can possibly prevent us from knowing and being all that this Self would have us know and be, except our own unregenerateness; and all this shall give way, and the right, our own loftiest will, shall triumph.

We all know better than we do. This book appeals to every one to begin, to persist in the realization of the ethical ideal; for the regeneration of society is to come about through education from within, not through correction from without Begin, live, aspire, realize, the best ideal of the moment; and this earnest effort shall lead the way to greater achievement. For every higher leads to the highest, and even the ethical life receives its crowning glory through the transcendent beauty of the spiritual. There is just as much need of a better form of religion, as a practical living essence beating in the heart of society, as there is of a higher ideal of justice and of business.

I am ready, in the full sense of the word, only for the step which logically follows the one I am just now taking. I must not overreach nor get into a nervous strain. I must not let my thoughts dwell on the future. I must not be anxious nor assert my own will, for I do so at the peril of my health and hap-piness. I ought rather to live in the eternal now, and to understand my expe-rience in the light of cause andeffect. I must build my new future by gradual modification of the present.

Experience

Whatever lies beyond human experience is most certainly an un-known world, and this statement applies with particular emphasis to the facts of our inner life. The ravings of the maniac are for him matters of expe-rience, for the moment emphatically real; and, lo cure him, it is necessary to broaden his experience. In the long run we know ourselves through remem-bered experience. What we mean by space, time, God, the universe, man, is so many ideal constructions from experience; for the world or any given ob-ject in it, and our ripened and classified knowledge of it, were not thrust up-on the mind ready-made from infancy. The race has learned from long ob-servation, based on repeated experience, that bodies everywhere occupy space, that time is required for growth and for the accomplishment of any physical operation, and that no event, however slight its importance, hap-pens uncaused.

The one great effort of truth-loving man is to learn what actually exists around him, and to describe it as one would picture an emotion or a beautiful landscape, so that another will know what the emotion means or will recog-nize the landscape when it is seen.

A dreary round for some, a relentless mystery for others, a paradox of sorrow and pleasure, of sin and saintliness, — where all endeavor is vain and all moralizing tedious, — experience leaves some characteristic and individual impression upon all. Some have been soured by it, some elevated and purified. Seek out the temper of the observers, and you shall find a miracle of difference separating two people who have faced parallel facts. Prosaic minds ask, Is life worth living? The poet blesses fate that he is permitted to exist.

The term "experience" exhausts all that we mean by life, the universe and God; for we only know of things, of the world, of persons, or even the higher spiritual illuminations, in so far as they come within experience, — that is, within feeling, thought, and will. Experience is thus a boundless whole whose basis is to be sought in the realm of the unseen or eternal, and it is intelligible to us in proportion to our three-fold understanding of it. All that we have seen, all that we have touched, handled, heard, suffered, enjoyed, loved, desired, and thought, all that we are as human beings, belongs here. Experience in the profoundest sense is one; for we never escape from it, nor are our faintest emotions separated from this infinite whole.

To know the Whole as it is progressively revealed in experience is the eternal truth. Again and again all that we seek to know, all that we seek to be, is made manifest. Again and again it presents itself for recognition to us; and we pass it by, because we have wrong ideas as to its place and nature. We have tried to square the world to our ideas of it: it is now time to make our consciousness conform to that which eternally exists.

There is another and a grander realm of experience lying beneath the shifting phenomena of mind and matter. To know it and to learn what our total experience means, we must come to judgment in our souls, come face to face with the finite self in all its simplicity, and seek there — in the domain of consciousness — the way of escape into the Spirit which holds all that is so paradoxical to the intellect in one completed experience where harmony prevails.

Slowly the lifelong process begins of distinguishing reality from illusion, the outer world from the inner, fate from freedom; and at every stage this development is made possible by one factor alone, — namely, mind, conscious mind seeking to grasp lifers great meaning. We cannot too often remind ourselves that without the cultivated ability to construct the world intelligibly in consciousness, without mind, thought, reason, the world would still be for us the confused whole of infancy.

Such help we should expect from perfect love and wisdom as should really further our progress without defeating the object of experience, just as we leave the child to work out a mathematical problem instead of solving it for him, when the child will obviously be the gainer. The Absolute Self might thus be present in our suffering in so far as our life experience is viewed as a progressively completed whole. Such a life as this — the life of the Absolute, where our tasks play their part in his larger experience — would be the completion of goodness as we know it, just as it is the completion of personality, of truth, beauty, life on all its planes, and of any particular end in the universe.

It becomes clear that virtue or goodness can only be attained through an experience full of contrasts and friction, an experience which calls out the best that is in us, — true Sympathy, love, and character. The meaning of man's own mysterious past becomes clear. He sees the rich compensation for all that he has suffered in the wisdom and character it has brought him. And, finally, in this far-reaching adjustment of means to ends he recognizes the love of God, and proves to his own satisfaction that love really dwells at the heart of the universe.

Suffering, then, is intended to make man think. Behind all experience moves one great aspiring Power, developing and perfecting the world. It moves straight toward its goal unceasingly and without permanent hindrance. Wherein man is adjusted to it, he is already free from suffering. He moves with it, and knows how to be helped by it. But, wherein he still acts ignorantly, he suffers, and is obviously sure to be in conflict until he understands the law of growth.

Our experience of today is conditioned by our past life. It is what we have passed through which alone makes it possible for us to stand where we do today. Consequently what we do and think today will largely govern our experience of tomorrow and of all future days. Fate has not decided everything for us after all; for it was by our own consent, unconsciously, thoughtlessly, and consciously, that we suffered. Our fate is that through our individuality something is bound to come forth, for the resistless power of Almighty God is behind it. Our freedom lies in choosing whether to move with progress or against it; for man may evidently continue to sin, to oppose, and misuse the very power that would bless him, and to postpone the lesson which at sometime and somewhere he is fated to learn.

When we cease to look upon any experience as too hard, we have made a decided step in wise adjustment to life. Life itself becomes easier and happier when we make this grand discovery that within each human soul there is a sufficient resource for every need along the line of the individual career.

What is the real meaning and purpose behind all these mysterious experiences and trials? Is it not the development of a soul, and is it not for lack of spiritual self-possession that we are whiffed about by opinions and fears? What is a soul? One may as well try to define the larger Self, from whom, as we are persuaded, the soul's noblest aspirations come. Yet we know perfectly well what we mean until we are asked to define it; and we have some conception of that eternal realm of thought, superior at once to space and to time, where the poets and philosophers dwell who speak words of comfort to the soul. Our own deepest reflection transports us there, and we seem larger as a result of our meditation.

24

Every trying experience demands a strengthening of one's faith or a deepening of one's self-possession; for the natural tendency is to fear, worry, and doubt. We are not sure of ourselves until we have met and undergone the test of a severe experience. Any experience, then, that strengthens this inward repose is rather a blessing than a hardship. Is it too much to say that we can become equal to any experience whatever, and meet it unmoved within, in quiet trust and perfect faith? Surely, the possibility is worthy of our consideration.

Conduct

All conduct should therefore be such that one could confess it fully without shame, — conduct in which the moral agent owns no allegiance to selfish interests, wherein one never bows to power nor worships partisan creeds, but where fully, freely, and courageously one could lay bare all that one is, all that one does and thinks, before Almighty God.

The ethical life is as simple as the spiritual which completes it. It is life worthy of being universal, it is sincerity, justice, truth, goodness, and beauty realized according to eternal law. It is a life wherein we do the best we can in the light of our highest insight. It only asks of us to give our souls, and not trade in appearances; but it asks this much of every man that lives.

Experience, tempered by reason, enlightens even the conscientious man, and guides him away from extremes; for one may easily become morbidly conscientious.

Always, then, the whole man should speak through a genuine moral action. One should make the best use of both intuition and reason, since both are needed to maintain the ethical balance.

Self-sacrifice at its best means the wise use of all that we are. In so far as it involves self-neglect, self-surrender, and self-suppression, it is sure to result in ill. The truly ethical man may, it is true, lay down his life for humanity, but he lays it down that he may find it enriched and more wisely directed on a higher plane.

The religious "ought" is the highest duty of all, since it includes and supplements all that is most vital in the righteous life. And by this we mean that spirit which makes the ethical life something more than the mere performance of duty. It amounts to worship and fervor for the right and true, — that state where the soul is really and deeply touched both with pity for humanity and by a desire to make man's condition better. It is the living essence which, by the majority of men, is simply accepted theoretically.

The essential in every case is to await the dictates of the inner sense, and then act rationally, faithfully, and trustfully, with the conviction that the right and the true will conquer in the end despite the firm hold of vice, injustice, and oppression, and with the knowledge that some high end will be accom-

25

plished through us, even though we are ignorant of it at the time; for the central point is ever to think and act in harmony with the higher self.

Self-scrutiny and consciously chosen goals may help us along the pathway of progress; but the greatest achievement in the end, the greatest sacrifice, the greatest freedom, is realized in the supreme choice, whereby one decides once for all to follow the divine life. This goal is alone complete and final, — complete through the steps that have led up to it, — it is that alone which we realize because we must, because thought itself can go no higher.

It is for us, if we would grow strong in the Spirit, to live a simple life, that nothing may interfere with the steady advance of the higher nature from within. Where the heart is right, all good works shall follow as the fruition of natural law. Where the heart is right, one may save one's self a thousand trying experiences, thereby making one's life far more helpful to others.

And, where the heart is right, a love that is superior to ourselves will choose us as its instruments in the expression of its own divinity.

No greater precept is emphasized by such soul communion than this: to keep the ideal ever before us, even when engaged in the most trivial task of patient, orderly realization of this perfect design of God. No greater mistake could be made than to confuse time and eternity, and declare all this to be accomplished now. He who really loves truth, law, and order, will throw himself in line with this highest moving, content if each day witnesses its triumph, its growth, and its act of service.

By thus squaring accounts with one's self, by individual thinking and self-reliance, one learns to remain at home in one's own soul. One learns to work and perceive with the soul, to give of one's self, to think, live, speak, and write with power. Onedoes not "descend to meet," nor is one narrowed by occupation or environment. One remains true to the inner self by maintaining this high level, and drawing all things up to that. Development, therefore, proceeds from within, each year in closer affinity with the Spirit.

For, obviously, there is no half-way position for those who thus comprehend life's unity. Every moment of existence must be a worship, every activity must be dedicated to the right, since one simple test is to be applied in all matters of conduct and in all great problems of philosophy; namely, Is this harmonious with the insight of my highest self?

Every act of conduct is due to a direction of mind; and the mind shapes the conduct, and draws to itself whatever corresponds to the thought, just as truly and in the same way as a magnet attracts particles of iron. As this may not be fully evident, it is well to consider the influence of thought at some length; for in this neglected factor of human experience we shall find the greatest help in the problems of health and happiness.

It is rather better to be tolerant, to have a large charity for people, than to expect them to be like ourselves. One person of a kind is usually enough. God apparently needs us all. Those who have learned to think, especially those who realize the meaning of evolution, are usually aware of their faults; and encouragement is what they most need. People do nearly as well as they can under the circumstances and with their scant wisdom. If we know a better way, it will become evident to them if we practice it.

An impulse blesses or curses, according to the opinion of it, the attitude toward it, and the way in which it is followed, blindly or intelligently. Man never conquers himself by self-suppression any more than by indulgence, but by adjustment to the forces of his own being.

We are too active as a rule, too sure of our own way, too much absorbed in our own plans and fears. The Spirit demands but little of us, quiet, lowly listening; but it does ask this much. Here is the real power and value of silence. All that we perceive in these happy moments spent in quiet reflection has a lasting effect upon us. It is then that we grow. It is then that ideals take shape, and become permanent directions of mind. It is then that we get newly adjusted to life; for, after all, this task is never completed. Something new and perplexing is ever coming to
test us; and always there is this one resource, to find our inward center, and there to stand firm and contented.

Conduct reduces itself to one simple rule: Study to know when you are moving along the lines of your own deepest nature, your own keenest sense of what is wise and. right, and when you are off the track. It is right and necessary to have certain standards by which conduct may be judged, to have a philosophy which teaches one to look on all sides of an issue and to reason carefully. It is well to look to friends, to public teachers and books, for help in all humility and willingness to learn. But standards vary. The conscience of a people changes from age to age. Even intuition must be verified. It must find support in reason, and undergo the test of experience. The surest and simplest method, for those who have become aware of such guidance, is to await the divine emphasis, to act when the whole being speaks, to move along those lines in which no faculty of one's being interposes an obstacle. All ultimate questions of right and duty should obviously be settled within the sacred limits of one's own personality, where the great God speaketh, if he speaks at all.

We owe it to ourselves, to our neighbor, to the universal brotherhood or the divine fatherhood, to be doing something in particular all the time, to choose this line of conduct and reject that. And this knowledge of duty should rest on a scientific interpretation of the universe, on a study of life in its total relations, including the discovery, so far as we can make it, of whither events are tending.

This doctrine, then, says in a word, Be unselfish; have an ideal outlook; see yourself as you would like to be, healthy, happy, well adjusted to life, helpful, wisely sympathetic, and ever ready with an encouraging word, looking for the good, growing strong in wisdom and power, patiently awaiting occasions, yet always sufficiently occupied, so that you will have no time to be annoyed, fearful, restless, or morbid. It points out new ways in which we can be of service to our fellow-men. It makes us aware of our own responsibility, and shows us that life is an individual problem. It warns us never to look upon that problem as too difficult to solve, if we approach it moderately, hopefully, and full of cheer.

What I am thinking and doing day by day is resistlessly shaping my future, — a future in which there is no expiation except through my own better conduct. No one can save me. No one can live my life for me. It is mine for better or for worse. If I am wise, I shall begin today by the simplest and most natural of all processes to build my own truer and better world from within. As surely as the great world of human thought comes round to the position of one man, so surely does the whole fabric of personal thought and action respond to our will. We have only to wait, to be patient, to renew our ideals day by day, to remember that ideas have life, regenerative life, and a natural law of growth. Nature and our own subconscious mind will do the work for us.

We often falsely accuse ourselves of sin, when the relapse is really due to a firm determination to be better. If we keep the end in view, if we have an ideal outlook, we can safely let the disturbance be what it may. Quiet persistence is the word. Each effort to renew our ideal adds to its evolutionary power.

Adjustment to life, then, is an individual problem, and varies with temperament, surroundings, and habits of thought. Its principles are universal. First to realize that there is but one Reality, or God; that we live in God; that God lives in us; that he is completing us, moving upon us through the forces, the events, the world in which he resides, through our weaker nature, through our faults, through the conflicts which we have so long misinterpreted, through pain, through happiness, and all that constitutes experience; that we have no power wholly our own, but that we use and are used by divine power; that we are equal to any task, any emergency, any struggle, for that great Reality is all there is. It is all power. God is here. Help is near. We need not go anywhere for it. It is omnipresent. It abounds. It comes to us in proportion to our receptivity to it, our faith in it, our happiness, our hope, our patience. Then to choose wisely what we wish to be in cooperation with the immanent Life, since "whatever determines attention determines action"; to see one's self not in the introspective, but in the divine light; to be practical in the choice of ideals.

Chapter Two

Will

The most difficult problem in the adjustment to life is, in fact, the right use and development of the will, to know just how far to cultivate the indomitable energy or persistence which lies at the foundation of success, to exercise the right amount of self-affirmation and reliance, and yet to avoid undue intrusion of one's personality; in a word, to avoid the extremes of asceticism, submission, and resignation, on the one hand, and the continual grasping for that which we neither need nor deserve on the other. The middle course is the true exercise of will-power or freedom. The extremes are profoundly selfish. No one can be truly engaged in the task of harmonious self-development and devoted labor for the good of humanity who has not met this fundamental question of the two selves, or wills, and reached some decision.

It is a necessity of our finite life to will something in particular, and whatever we really love or will we habitually seek. To think that all ambition must be crushed out, the individuality suppressed, and this world's goods discarded simply because they are not spiritual, is obviously to fall into a great error. There is a wrong and a right self-sacrifice, as we shall see later. Whatever individuality and energy we possess should no more be scorned than intellect or reason, for self-suppression inevitably brings about a reaction. True individuality, the right use of every thing and every power we possess, is no more incompatible with obedience to the higher will than fate is incompatible with freedom. It is one's true wisdom both to conquer one's nature and to obey it, to win self-mastery not through resignation, not by killing out desire, but through obedience and co-operation; for every faculty is good, if wisely used.

Behind the stream of consciousness is the human will, choosing and giving shape to it. The direction of mind is the tendency which gives shape to physical, intellectual, moral, and spiritual conduct. The idea is the foremost factor in every aspect of experience. These two facts namely, that the infinite Power is trying to make something of us through our individuality, and that everything, happiness, misery, health, and disease, depends on our attitude toward that Power — explain the very mysteries of suffering and evil, at least so far as our limited knowledge can make them clear.

By saying, "I will do this," "I will have things thus and so," we are apt to get into a nervous strain, to assert our own power, our own selfishness, as though the human will were all-powerful. Self-conceit and ignorance of the larger and diviner life accompany such self-assertion, and close the door to the higher power. The Spirit quietly withdraws at the approach of such assertion.

Will is a direction of mind with a definite object in view. It is the mental or conscious side of physical conduct, and as such it wields great power. It is thought filled in and calling force into a given channel. Will uses power. It gives definite shape to power. It opens one to power, so that "I will" is equivalent to "I am ready." A person with a strong will is one who persistently keeps a desired object in view. The human power lies in the desire, the divine or natural in that which fulfills it. Here is a very important distinction. By longing for an object we unconsciously put ourselves in an attitude to attain it. We gravitate toward it. We exclude everything else in our efforts to attain it All else is merely overdoing the
matter.

Desire

To desire the ideal, the true, the good, for its own sake, is to become aware that in our deepest Self we already possess it. Human experience is a progressive discovery or consciousness of that which is eternal. It is the eternal in detail, in time and space relations. Desire indicates the presence of that which seeks fulfillment through us. It is the ideal dwelling in and transmuting the so-called real, it is the purpose of the completed self. It is not, therefore, the personal self alone. That which knows its own end, through us of course knows how to fulfill that end.

Life gains wonderfully in attractiveness as soon as one ceases to plan for the universe. It is enough for me to be responsible for myself. By putting an end to this constant reaching out for somewhat that we do not deserve, by reducing all desires to a few commendable ideals, and by becoming quietly contented, the real worth of life has an opportunity for the first time to make itself perceived. The Master of events has been capable of planning for us all along, but we have somehow deemed it best to take the affair into our own hands. The power of affinity or desire will attract such Mends, such opportunities and possessions, as we need, if we give it freedom to act. The law that nature seeks the simplest course, or the line of least resistance, applies with equal force to the mental realm. And this restful attitude of mind — ever ready to do the task at hand, but never seeking more than our own inmost spirit attracts — is so effective that no other reaction upon life is to be compared with it.

Silently and unobserved, the Spirit will breathe upon us if we reflect, if we wait for it in stillness day by day. It will not come if we doubt, if we fear, or — note this especially — if our own thought be too active; for the Spirit never intrudes.

Attention

The art of remembering well depends largely on the attention one gives to a speaker or book. That speaker or book is interesting which wins and holds our attention. That thought or event influences us which makes an impression, and becomes part of our mental life through the attention. We learn a language, grasp some profound philosophy, or experience the beneficial effect of elevating thought, rid ourselves of morbid, unhealthy, or dispiriting states of mind with their bodily expressions, in proportion as we dwell on some ideal or keep before us some fixed purpose, until by persistent effort the goal be won.

Intuition

The purer the insight, so much the less of personal desire and preconception does it contain. Intellectual perception and prejudice relate to the individual, and depend on the knowledge gained through past experience. But true insight is of the universal, relates to the general good, and is most likely to come to those whose motives are purest, who possess due receptivity, humility, and willingness to recognize a higher self, and that fine discrimination which separates personal inclination from duty.

The chief task in early life is to discover one's leading talent, to rely upon it, cultivate it, and learn to know how to follow its intuitive guidance. There is no surer pathway to true success, true originality and freedom, than to follow this native leading along the lines and under the conditions in which it most readily sheds its light. Intuition in this sense is emphatically personal or individual. It is the instinct of character, of talent and genius, and naturally differs in each individual. In the last analysis, then, what one frequently means by faith or intuition is one's self or soul; and one could no more convey it to another than one could communicate one's soul.

He who devotes himself to the higher life therewith receives help in proportion to his receptivity. One might then seem to have special guidance, when, as a matter of fact, one's life is simply in closer sympathy with the higher law, and is therefore guided according to the needs of the life of self-sacrifice. The light, the guidance, the power, exist for all who are willing to make the sacrifice.

But a time comes when purely personal plans, desires, and ambitions seem like mere by-play as compared with this direct leading from within. One may still devise, plot, and build air-castles, if one will; one may examine a proposed line of conduct in the light of prudential and financial reasons. Yet one cannot escape the conviction that all this is superficial amusement, and is only needed when one is not yet sure of the higher guidance. For all who can detect the higher moving there is, in fact, just one way to the solution of all difficulties: put yourself in quiet, expectant, trustful harmony with the inner tendency, and await its guidance.

It is not, then, the experience of occasional impressions and guidances which makes intuition very nearly the most real of all life's gifts, but the continuity, the harmony, and equanimity of this ever-present and all-knowing self, before which all other selves pale into their true significance. One feels indubitably sure that life is made of one hidden piece, that a somewhat presides over its events, in whose wisdom one may trust, and that life as a whole has a meaning, a purpose, wherein all things, all so-called happenings, all aspirations, belong together, and where there is a steady march of events toward the great goal of the universe.

This guidance enters into the minutest details. Circumstances are adjusted, people come forward to play their part, one is made ready intellectually and spiritually, and nothing at times seems more certain than the prearrangement by a higher power of every moment of experience.

Not until I compare the lowest with the highest self do I perceive the difference between the divine and human intuitions. Then I discover that the impersonal or higher intuition is the blending point of two worlds, or aspects of the divine self-manifestation. Above and beyond extends the living Reality itself. Beneath is the world of by-play, of finite amusement and speculation, pleased with itself, fond of its own paradoxes and its lengthy disquisitions wherein the reality is simply talked about. Above exists the great unit, a single voice, a single guidance, unmistakable, unwavering, persistent, teleological.

Intuition may, in fact, be compared to the pure ideal of God, the completed whole, the eternal now, while reason is its systematic and detailed development in the realm of space and time. Once more one discovers the great twofold experience, involution and evolution, substance and form, subject and object, ideal and realization, vision and interpretation, feeling and thought, abstract and concrete, desire and fulfillment, mysticism and philosophy, as so many members of one whole. He is well balanced who sees that the two are bound each to each by ties of eternal necessity, and that one may not safely develop in the one direction without a corresponding development in the other.

It is a universal failing of those who take intuition for their guide to become dogmatic. Intuition alone, in this early stage, is even more deceptive than reason, because it is credulous, while reason is more cautious and discerning. It is not enough to state things on authority, nor can insight safely be accepted in the simple form in which it comes. Beware, then, of every one who lays down the law, who says unqualifiedly reality is this or spirituality is that, because he feels it to be thus and thus. Some one else may declare it to be the reverse. It is one thing to have an experience or illumination, and quite another thing to interpret it correctly. Every statement, whether rational or intuitive, necessarily falls short of the reality. It can only be true at best to an aspect or phase of life, and should be received with suspicion if it purports to be more. It is the intuition or immediate experience often times that is true, not the statement of it; and, whenever intuition is associated with dogma, it may safely be taken with a grain of allowance, if not rejected as utterly spurious.

The danger of following intuition too far is once more apparent to everybody who has carefully noted the mental difference between man and woman. With all due respect to the insight revealed in "woman's reason," — and it is evident that it should be trusted by man far oftener than it is, — it is well known that its emotional accompaniment befogs the judgment, makes one too susceptible, and clearly shows the lack of the one common meeting-point and firm foundation of finite intelligence, — reason. As a rule, woman needs reason as much as man lacks spiritual insight; and the crying need of all who would be well developed intellectually, morally, and spiritually, is the harmonious and simultaneous development of both.

There is a conviction born of experience interpreted by reason which no analysis can measure. It is like the electric spark which unites oxygen and hydrogen by some mystical process into something totally different called water. We are convinced by something higher than ourselves, something that knows us, that reaches the burning point for a moment in our inmost consciousness, and then leaves us to study the impression left upon us. When we rationalize it we may fully trust it. In a deeper sense, to understand it in full, one must be that which illumines, that self-existent Unity whence springs the twofold experience of our human life.

Intuition is bound up with the personality, and what seems to be a guidance or inspiration is often the mere quickening of the divine ideal. The soul sees and knows immediately because it is just that ideal, events are adjusted, and the way made open because a higher Power is working through us.

Open your soul to illumination in its purest form, trust your insight, your faith, your strong impression, believe in it, let it have spontaneous expression through you as though you really believed it to be a perfect law, watch for it, await its coming, and give it a most thorough test. The experiment is worth the while, even when we know not whence our daily bread is coming from, and when we "take no thought for the morrow."

Those who seek such guidance must therefore pay its price. The first step is to desire it, to believe that it is competent to provide for all real needs, and to discover how we have all the time unconsciously used it while attributing its help to other sources. The next step is to brush aside the great mass of debris which has so long obscured the tiny tendrils of this fairest growth of the higher life, to forego this endless pursuit of self, of pleasure and gain, — in a word, to cultivate a simple life. Our complex modem life, with its innumerable cares and interests, leaves no moment free for genuine spiritual growth. The greatness, the wisdom and strength, of intuition, lie in its simplicity. It possesses and will teach the soul in a few short sentences the very essence of all that is true and valuable in the much-lauded wisdom of men. It is the pith, the spirit and beauty of life; it is love, goodness, gentleness, and humility itself, and humility must seek out its own most original way to the secrets and power at its command.

A new interest and pleasure are added to life for all whose desire it is to conform their lives to its sublime dictates. Everything in life takes on the hue of the divine in-shining. It paints the world in colors of rarest beauty and radiance, suffusing a charm where all seemed mean and despicable before. It compels one to be an optimist, to have faith in the eternal goodness of the universe, to believe in fate, and love the omnipresent Father. It will not always illumine the soul when one most desires it. We need all the guidance we can get from other sources. We need self-reliance and unflinching energy. Above all, we must be sure that the guidance is genuine. But doubt it as we may, wander off its narrow pathway as we may, it is ever there. When it presents no obstacle, we are free to act,

When it guides, there is no greater happiness than to obey.

Tolerance

As a matter of fact, we seldom know enough about people to praise or blame them. Their motives and duties in life are only partially known even to them. A whole social group may be apparently selfish, plutocratic, and indifferent as related to their immediate neighbors, yet be playing an unconscious and necessary part in the evolution of the race as a whole.

Apparently, we cannot be too tolerant of the methods of the universe nor too charitable toward those whose mission is a mystery to us, since we know too little as yet to view our social evolution as a whole or to apprehend its complete organization in a particular case.

Belief

The student of systematic thought, as he turns over the great books of the world, its varied philosophies of materialism, idealism, pantheism, and the rest; its innumerable religions, varying from fetishism, polytheism, and nature-worship to the great moral and spiritual doctrines of the East, all standing for some need, some aspiration and aspect of human society, all claiming to be true, yet all necessarily in some sense false; and even as he considers the variance of opinion among the relatively small body of nine-teenth-century scientists, — the student is awed by the wealth of human speculation and thought, and is almost at a loss to know what to believe about life and about men. For people accept the most incongruous beliefs with "smiling complacency." Side by side with the ardent believer, enslaved by a dogmatism which pretends to rest on an infallible revelation, one shall find the agnostic who is in doubt whether to believe at all. Personalities and personal emotions, prejudices and preconceptions, are often far more pow-erful factors than pure love of truth.

Chapter Three

Self

An endless variety of selves emerge from the mysterious realm of the subject, often times to the astonishment and wonder of the observer, — the physical ego, the social self, the self that is presented to one's kindred and the self that greets the stranger, the self that pretends to be happy when it is in truth thoroughly miserable, and that deeply reflective self which observes these petty egos, and tries to marshal them into some sort of consistency and frankness. As there is no hard and fast line between self and not-self, so there is no clear demarcation between the profound ego that knows and the varia-ble ego that is known. He is indeed fortunate who knows some one of his selves with sufficient thoroughness to establish it as a starting-point from which to comprehend the deep unity of them all.

If I could thus see myself as I fully am I should probably find myself as one among many individuals, standing for some idea which no other soul is so well adapted to represent, a character which all other souls probably share in their own way. It is enough for me to know that I am needed. Life can nev-er seem dull and unworthy of being so long as this consciousness persists. If I lose it, I have only myself to blame. I am fated to miss my true self until, hav-ing exhausted mere self-scrutiny, I await in silence, and let myself be discov-ered as a moment embosomed in eternity, a word in the divine language, a quality of purest absolute being. That which a moment before seemed hard and fast limitation now appears in its true light as an element of beauty, in-separably and intimately relating the finite to the infinite. No self is complete until it thus becomes self-conscious. No self is in full self-possession until it knows itself in God. Here is the true subject which never could become ob-ject, for finite self-analysis; for, if it could, we should cease to be finite. Here is the joyous passage into the divine.

The self of any given moment is like the experience of the bee imprisoned for an instant in the honey-laden flower and oblivious of the great world outside. The bee hums onward to the next flower; and so do I to my next moment, all the while cherishing up the memory of these successive steps. I long to grasp all these moments in their unity, but now at last I know a Self that can grasp them. If at one moment I seem puny and ignorant, at another — in the ineffable moment of illumination — I am the heir of all the ages and of all wisdom. In these two moments I know myself first as finite, then as infinite.

In those quiet hours of reflection when the soul searches for tell-tale traces of itself, it suddenly flashes upon the mind that one has hitherto lived merely for self. Then how mean, infinitesimal, despicable, seems the life one has lived in comparison to the larger life of service and self-denial which now for the first time presents itself in all its beauty to the thought I All sermons, all good intentions, and all efforts to make one's self believe that one really is not selfish are fruitless up to this point. One really has not begun to live until now. Experience in the past was so much half-wasted preparation and indefinite postponement of life's great lesson. Now life begins to be thoroughly worth the living, and the continual ennui of existence at last ceases forever.

Self-analysis will lead one more into self or far out beyond it, according to the degree of penetration. To stop half-way is to become imprisoned in the purely finite self, and to live in distasteful proximity to one's sensations. To live as much above the conscious process as possible, while still carrying it on and making the best use of it, marks a well-poised mind.

No man can tell another all that he perceives there in the secret place of the
heart where one is caught up into the heaven of the larger Self. But the conviction grows with years, and the joy deepens with every fresh experience that the Father really knows us in these rare moments as a needed part of his own being. Self-consciousness at its best is thus self-recognition of the Absolute. It is the finite and infinite made momentarily one. It is the soul's solution of the great question which is next to engage our attention, — the discovery of the ultimate Reality toward which experience points through all the avenues of feeling and thought.

For here, on the one hand, is that Self whom no words can adequately name, whom no thought can grasp, whom no life, no world, no universe, seems wholly to reveal, who is no less, but infinitely more, than we mean by the words person, universe, mind, beauty, power, goodness, Spirit, God, Father, or any term that has been rightfully applied to him in the past. Yet, on &e other hand, the finite self is still there, one with, but not identical with, the ineffable Spirit, so that in this sublime moment one is apparently — yes, one is deeply and truly — this absolute Self, in part, beholding its well-ordered system of self-manifestation.

The finite self, broadly cultivated, is the clew to the secret of the universe. The mystic misses its beauty on the one side through lack of discrimination, the scientific specialist on the other because the spiritual sense has not been quickened.

I understand so far as I have thought. My perception of the world is partly myself. My most secret and personal thought is partly a superior intuition. Guidance, desire, will, faith, illumination, — all this is in turn partly myself, my temperament, character, experience, and personality, and partly the purpose, the will, and wisdom of God.

Impartially and freely the superior Self bestows its bounties upon the listener in proportion to his worth, his ability to absorb and give forth, and his receptivity, or willingness to withdraw his own opinion. On the one hand, the in-shining is divine and infallible; on the other, by becoming human, it partakes of the limitations of the recipient.

Self exists within self, — the social self, the self of impulse and emotion, and the self of reason, the conscious self and the subconscious, wherein we turn over and view ideas in all their aspects until they become fixed habits of thought, the fleeting ephemeral self which reveals itself in an endless variety of moods, opinions, and feelings, and the permanent self which we call soul, that deeper consciousness which blends with the Self of selves.

But some self is always uppermost. To this we are for the moment devoted; and it is this more superficial self or direction of mind that we are most concerned with in daily life.

One's method of adjustment to life or one's optimism need not necessarily be the philosophy of this book. There are as many approaches to it as there are temperaments, and this is just the point of this chapter. Have a method. Have a soul of your own. Be your true self. Think, realize, reflect, until you have a measure of unborrowed conviction, which establishes a center of repose, and is a source of happiness and contentment, — a center which yields to no outer tumult, but is ever receptive to the divine Self; which never harbors fear or doubt, no matter what the wavering self may say.

Asceticism

His conclusion is, therefore, that "the highest moral end is self-realization"; for he recognizes only himself, all else is illusion. He thus revolves around the center of his own finite consciousness, and consequently he leads the egoistic life of asceticism, — a life closely bordering upon selfishness in its worst form. For the tendency is to emphasize the impersonal; to dwell upon the All and the Absolute until the finer human emotions are crushed out, and one neglects the little acts of kindness and sympathy which lie at the basis of true friendship.

The wrong idea of self-abnegation not only leads to the selfish life of asceticism and the infliction of bodily harm, the partial loss of individuality — which should not be sacrificed under any circumstances — and the surrender of laudable ambition, but it really prevents one from accomplishing the greatest good, since the right use of all that we have and of all that we can become through harmonious self-development is thoroughly compatible with the highest usefulness.

Fear

It is a revelation to most people to discover the power of fear in their own lives. It enters into their religion. It often inspires the prejudice which stifles unbiased inquiry. It enters into every detail of daily life. We are apprehensive, as a race. We picture calamities of every description, and dread the worst. The sensational press furnishes constant material for fear. We fear to eat this and that. We dread, anticipate, and really put ourselves in the best attitude to take certain diseases; and we live in constant fear of death. And fear is simply another form of opinion. It runs back to our willingness to believe rather than to think for ourselves. It is based on ignorance, increases in intensity with the degree of superstition, and vanishes when we understand the law of development, of cause and effect.

If we fear, we open ourselves to all sorts of fancies, which correspond to our thought, and cause them to take shape. If we communicate our fears to friends, their thought helps ours. If we get angry, jealous, act impetuously, we suffer just in proportion to our thought. If we pause to reflect, to wait a moment in silence, until we are sure of our duty, we experience the benefit of quiet meditation.

We invite what we expect. We attract what we are like. Let one understand this, and one need never fear.

It should not therefore be a new source of terror to learn that we are beset by all sorts of subtle influences and hypnotic forces, or to be told that our own thought directions are largely instrumental in causing misery, dis-ease, and trouble of all sorts. These wrong influences cannot touch us. Our own mental atmosphere, our whole being, is a protection against them, if we have reached a higher plane. There must be a point of contact in order for one mind to affect another, some channel left open, some sympathy, just as there must be a certain affinity in order for two persons to form a mutual friendship. Our safety, our strength, lies in knowing our weakness, in discovering that the law of direction of mind is fundamental in every moment of human life. If after that we go on in the same old way, complaining, fearing, thinking along narrow lines, and submissively accepting the teaching of others, it will not be because we do not understand the law.

Worry and fear play an important part in all varieties of disease, and some peoplehave scarcely a moment's freedom from some tormenting belief, or mental picture. Ill-will, want of charity, jealousy, anger, or any emotion which tends to draw one into self, to shut in and contract, is immediate in its effect;

for, if it be continued, it disturbs the whole being, it is reflected in the spiritual matter, and finally in the body, where it is treated as if it were a physical disease. Unrealized ambition, suppressed grief, continued unforgiveness, dwelling in grief and troubles, instead of living above them, disappointments, and a thousand unsuspected causes, which impede the free and outing expression of the individuality, have a corresponding effect on the outer being.

Doubt

He alone knows the Father to be literally the All who has given thought the utmost opportunity to doubt him, only to find that the mind is begirt on all sides by that which it would deny. Sound human ignorance to its ultimate depth, fearlessly, patiently, persistently, and you shall find that every item of doubt is at the same time an inexpressibly wealthy source of profound conviction: until the giant skepticism has been met and mastered in his own realm the human spirit has no genuine peace.

Whence came the universe, how came we by these unquenched longings, this restless search for truth, beauty, and virtue, this belief in a God, or Spirit, this rational demand for an ultimate ground of things, unless there is a deep unfathomed Self within, a fundamental Reality which already possesses this limitless experience of nature, of the social organism, and of self-consciousness in its completion? And, if this deeper Self within is identical with the Reality, or Life, which underlies all being without, must we not, then, enlarge our consciousness until it shall include the All in all, the eternal Beauty, and the immanent Father, knowing us as a part of himself, in one great living realization of his presence?

Slowly, patiently, but surely, thoroughly, and with an eternal fitness, a beauty of design and organization which have been the wonder of man ever since human thinking began, our world is nearing its completion as an organic part of a great stellar and planetary system. Slowly and with infinite care the complex organism of human society is learning its lesson, guided by forces which we see not, moving toward ends which are lost in an ideal future, and in every part, in every soul, in every struggling life, with you and with me, inspired, guided, and sustained by that Spirit which nothing can separate from us or from the world, since there is naught beside.

Here, at any rate, is the highest level we can now reach, where the finite soul no longer regards itself as the source of its best thoughts and its wisest deeds, where the soul could not doubt if it would since it is in the moment of complete self-renunciation, perhaps of utter despair and weakness that God at last makes himself really known. Thus in the moment of the profoundest agony, it may be, when the soul cries out in despair, "My God, my God, why hast thou forsaken me?" as in the moment of the sincerest skepticism and in the sublimest vision of the mystic, there is an assurance born of infinite wisdom and power, before which human will, human doubt, is powerless. The finite will in its utmost extremity confesses its weakness, losing itself to find itself again transfigured in the glory of the infinite.

Evil

"Evil is simply the lower state of living as looked at from the higher state." Let this principle be thoroughly understood once for all, and we shall have a clew to the interpretation of the darkest pages of life's history. For it is clear that the genuine truth-seeker can ignore no facts. Any doctrine which has won general acceptance contains an element of truth, — truth as seen from a particular point of view. And oftentimes there is no safer guide to the common ground of human experience than to study the most antagonistic views of it. Any truth, any experience, any fact or emotion, however true for us, needs its complement. Every man is in some respect incomplete, unbalanced, undeveloped; until he not only learns the great lesson of experience, — namely, wholeness, poise, beauty, harmony, — but actually, conscientiously, and persistently supplies what is lacking.

Side by side in one experience the utmost contrasts exist; and the soul, passing itself in review, turns from passions which link it to the brutes to virtues which make it the equal of angels. That which in other men constitutes their talent for business, art, music, poetry, even for sinfulness, self-assertion, and pessimism, exists also in the observer, but has never been emphasized or developed. In estimating the value of the whole, not one fact can be sacrificed.

Evil loses half its terrors for us when we thus view it in the light of the whole, and consign it to the lowest round in the ladder of being. We have had a false idea of life as a whole, and thought that evil should not exist at all, as though we could learn to know light without contrasting it with darkness. We have had a wrong idea of heaven, as a place where there should be nothing to overcome, nothing to win, and therefore nothing to sacrifice. Then, too, we have tried to exterminate evil instead of realizing that it is not in itself bad, but is really "the lower state of being looked at from the higher." We have dealt with society as though it were much further advanced in its evolution than it really is. The evils of intemperance in all its forms, and all the corruptions of government and society in our large cities, are the mud and mire of a civilization not yet emerged from the earth.

Nothing, then, is wholly what it appears to be by itself. Nothing is "sufficient unto itself" nor good by itself, — neither matter, mind, thought, feeling, nature, nor man. It is a slander upon our fair universe to speak of any one as totally depraved. It shows ignorance of our high origin to regard anything, any man, as independently good. Fitness to play one's part in the completion of some whole is ever the mark of goodness. A thing is bad or evil by excess

40

or defect: and the same thing may be both good and evil, according to the point of view.

Not to regard any tendency in one's self or in another as essentially evil, but as so much misdirected energy, deemed bad only because it is compared with a higher standard and because its use is not yet fully understood.

The meaning of much of our moral suffering and evil is, then, to teach the right use of our powers; and moral misery and degradation will probably continue until the lesson be learned. All cases of sickness, misery, evil, wrong, demand better self-comprehension. If there be one general meaning which applies to them all, it is, in one word, progress, — the effort of the Spirit to give us freedom. If we understood this, we should have a larger sympathy and charity for the whole human race, and be spared much suffering over the sins and crimes of others, and should look for the meaning, the Spirit, behind all wrong acts and all degraded lives.

No man, then, is inherently wicked. There are no heathen. No one is lost or ever could sink so low that the same Spirit that had a meaning in his sin could not carry him through it to a conscious realization of what that meaning is. Once more the vital question is, What is the divine meaning of it all? For, if a person or an act has a meaning, that person or deed is not and cannot be wholly evil, and to say that any act of wickedness happens despite the divine power is to deprive that power of the very infinity and wisdom by virtue of which both God and the universe exist.

Not every evil act has its discernible meaning. Most of our suffering is purely incidental, passing off without leaving us any the wiser; but all suffering, all evil, may become evolutionary. Every slightest experience will teach us something if we question it, and will yield its message of hope. This is the chief value of all experience and of the present discussion; for the final meaning of suffering is hope, the last word of this chapter is "hope," the message of the Spirit as it speaks ta us in moments of despair, in times of trouble, throughout life, throughout history, in all evolution, is a grand inspiring Hope.

Chapter Four

Personality

Personality is that character by which we distinguish one individual from another; and there must surely be a permanent essence there to which all that pours forth to the world of genius, of poetry, music, wisdom, and the spirit, is fundamentally attributable. Personality is thus of itself a whole, a miniature or epitome of all that is best in the life of the individual. It speaks above words, and rises superior to all analysis. Yet its essence refuses to be defined in purely finite terms. Indeed, when one turns aside from the outer world and clears away the accretions that have gathered about one's finitude, all that one finds there within is a vain shadow, like the dull reflection mirrored in the bottom of a well by which Lowell characterizes the shallow sentimentalists of the last century.

The great seers, Swedenborg and Emerson, the one with his discriminative doctrine of correspondences, of the need of both the divine love and the divine wisdom, and the other with his sublime doctrine of self-reliance, — the truth that each man stands for a particular fact, which no one else can understand as well, — thus include all that is best in mysticism without sacrificing the truth of personal relationship, of moral responsibility and growth. Both seers recognize the two sides, yet see their unity. And both have poetically suggested the divine and relatively unwordable communion of the lesser with the greater Self, or Oversoul, — a description in which mysticism is seen at its best, fulfilling the office which only seership can perform.

The difference between one person and another, then, is fundamental. One has only to try to put one's self in the mind of a friend in order to realize this wonderful difference. Let the friend be one's closest companion, one's mother or brother, whom one has known intimately from infancy; and even here the transition is impossible. There is something that we cannot grasp, because it is the Mend's experience, and can never be ours. Personality, — what is it, whence came it, and what does it mean?

One fact remains true of all personalities, however great the difference between them. They are all conscious beings. On the one hand come impressions from the world of matter. On the other come thoughts and influences in the sphere of mind. The two unite in consciousness, and form the world of mental life, or our interpretation of the great organized whole of which we are part In the center exists man. Looking one way, all that he sees is apparently material. Looking in the other, all appears to be mind. When he seeks their unity, he finds it alone in the conscious self which underlies them both, which therefore makes his whole life mental, and which is to be explained only by reference to the one Self.

Individuality

This deeper life in mind must then take the place of the superficial world of opinion. The dogmas and influences of other people must be rigorously excluded until, in moments of silence and quiet reflection, one learns the divine point of view through the individual man.

One may seriously question if the limitations of temperament will ever be overcome, if one man can ever describe life except as he sees it, modified by the general knowledge of the race. Perhaps that very feeling of individuality is fundamental in the thought of God, is the divine consciousness focalized in a given direction. If so, it is each one's duty to cultivate this profoundest individuality, and discover just what God means through it, what aspect of life one is best able to interpret.

Atmospheres

Every sensitive person is also aware of mental atmospheres surrounding persons and places, just as the odor emanates from and surrounds a rose. Wherever man has lived and thought, these atmospheres have been left behind him. They are associated with chairs where people have sat for some length of time. They are associated with clothing, and a change of clothing is therefore sufficient at times to change the state of mind.

Every sound makes an impression on the atmosphere capable of setting up a corresponding vibration in the ears of all who are within a certain distance. In a similar manner each thought is probably registered on this subtle ether; and those who are open to it through sympathy or some common interest become aware of it or unconsciously receive the benefit of it Minds of a like order are thus enabled to think together. The new thoughts of one stimulate those who are ready to respond, while thoughts that do not concern us pass off like sound in a desert, where there is no one to hear. Sympathy, receptivity, is the prime requisite in conscious thought communication. Yet, if there be an intermental substance, all minds must be open to it in some degree, and the most potent influences may be received unconsciously.

This ethereal substance in which our minds seem to be bathed is probably molecular in structure; yet it is obviously finer than electricity or the luminiferous ether, and is capable of penetrating the most minute spaces, just as the coarser gases interpenetrate the molecules of liquids and solids. It is evidently the finest grade of matter, and is immediately responsive to the slightest possible thought activity.

It is a well-known fact that during this subconscious process new light is thrown on difficult questions, and the perplexing problem which we dismiss from consciousness at night is often solved for us in the morning. Whence came the new solution? Have we not arrived once more at the general conclusion of this book; namely, that "we lie open on one side to the deeps of spiritual nature, to the attributes of God"? This openness is greater during sleep; and it is probably then that the mind gets many of its new ideas from the very source of wisdom, the mind that cannot change, the All-knowledge.

Fate

Is fate absolute? Then our attitude should be wise adjustment to it, with fate's ideal for our own, since it is a matter of economy to take life with the least degree of friction. Do we create our own fate? Once more it is a matter of economy and of necessity to have an ideal. Thus there is no escape from the conclusion that fate is not absolute, and that, however we regard it, — whether we accept freedom as a dictum of consciousness or believe that everything is determined even to the day of our death, — our ideas about it play some part in shaping our conduct, either through adjustment, through complaint and rebellion, or through co-operation; for we inevitably assume some habitual and effective attitude of mind toward it. This attitude, look at it as we may, is a conclusion, a deduction from experience; and our future conduct thus becomes the child of conscious choice.

No one possesses absolute freedom, and no one in our phase of life, who truly knows himself, is perfectly satisfied. But, if he labors because he is eager to perform a certain task, he acts to this extent of his own free will. So far as he rebels, he is again consciously exercising his freedom right, just as we are free to plan, to build air-castles and the like, when intuition tells us that all this is mere by-play as compared with the higher guidance. Experience can alone teach the true economy of life: it is our choice to continue to resist or freely to obey.

Obviously, there is no such thing as "luck" or chance in this reaction. If we persistently fail, the fault is in us. If we are uniformly successful, we may thank our own inner nature. Seek to evade the point as we may, the truth is forced upon us in the calm moments of self-consciousness that, however we may suffer or rejoice today, it is our own temperamental thought in the past that has sought out the way in which we are now traveling. We thus find ourselves creatures of our own fate, and in every instance the real authors of our own happiness and misery.

Life, in the main, so far as its general trend is concerned, was fated to be just as we find it, today; but within the limits, of the immutable . pathways of destiny it is clear that we possessed considerable freedom, and that of our own choosing we wandered here and there away from the narrow course of righteousness. And in this same calm moment the future opens up before us in two general directions; we find ourselves free to postpone our lesson, free to stray upon the by-paths of sin, self-seeking, and misery, or to find true freedom through obedience to the higher law.

Perhaps, after all, that man is freest who most faithfully moves with fate; while the slave is he who rebels, condemns the universe, and persistently disregards the dictates of conscience. Perhaps the freedom to which we aspire is that complete harmony of the human with the divine will which makes one particular line of conduct incumbent upon us in preference to a thousand others. Perhaps, too, in those moments of supreme decision, when we choose whom and what we shall serve, when we seem to be most truly ourselves by virtue of the clear exercise of reason and spiritual insight, we are, as Swedenborg maintained, really acted upon, although we seem to be making the choice ourselves.

The rigid fate brought upon us by our own acts is thus the precise experience through which true freedom and virtue are at last obtained. All is mysterious and regrettable until we come to judgment. Then the man who truly knows himself finds it impossible to regret a single act. On the one side, every moment of our past life seems to have been either chosen at random or determined. On the other, it is clear that we were wiser than we knew; for all these incidental details, these decisions and conscientious reactions, have somehow played their part in a drama designed by a higher intelligence than our own. Finally, then, we are convinced that in the divine economy no detail is lost. Whatever we choose shall be turned to account. Whatever we choose will teach us its lesson — when we learn to think. And whatever we choose is not, after all, selected at random; for the chooser is in his deepest life an immortal spirit, an organ of the infinite Self, so that the only just estimate of any detail, however trivial, is that which considers it in the light of the Whole.

Every moment of our actively conscious life, from morning to night, from infancy to old age, is governed by some act of will: we are paying attention to this particular object in the field of vision to the exclusion of many others, we are directing our energies along certain channels instead of innumerable others which we were free to choose; for will or love is the specific direction of mind which marshals and gives shape to details.

Law, purpose, will, fate of some kind, is involved in every event of life; and it depends upon our conscious attitude toward it whether it finds us a freeman or a slave. All causation, all change, is a matter of minute modifications, brought about, not through interference from without, but through law as a direct out-growth or immanent quickening of that which already exists. Fate therefore gives us freedom, at least relatively, as a part of the great moral purpose of the universe, by imposing upon us certain conditions.

I like to believe that the guidances of the spiritual sense are the foreshadowings of immovable fate, and that the right, the true, and the good will conquer in the end by inexorable law. But the incidents or means by which the end is attained are by no means final. Deeper than these, beneath all determinism, is the will or love by which it is established. There is nothing more fundamental than this.

Not until one is fully ready to co-operate is the will wholly thrown with the higher self or the lower self, as the case may be; and this casting of the balance on the one side or the other, this co-operation with that which frees or that which imprisons, may often depend on the merest caprice, — even the daring to disobey conscience, that in the fire of remorse one may at last know the heart of the moral life. And these preferences, these whims, loves, and desires are only to be unified or explained at last on the supposition that something profounder than all this means one persistent idea through all that passes under the name of determinism.

And a time will come when the higher life is no longer a theory, but an actual fact; and, with this higher consciousness, all friction between the two wills ceases. One no longer cares to choose and plan. One freely and fully decides once for all to obey the law, and let one's energy co-operate with the life that is all of one piece. It is then at last that one truly becomes a center of power, a magnet to attract those whom one can serve, and a conscious spiritual agent, not through mystical absorption, but through intelligent understanding that one is an organ of the divine nature, of that which is in its essence free.

The universe is intelligible to man in so far as he discovers the fundamental unity of the two opposed wills, the harmony of fate and freedom: his life is virtuous and a benefit to his fellow-men to the degree that the lower is brought round into harmony and co-operation with the higher. There are two wills when and to the degree that man considers himself alone. There is one Will, one fate, one destiny, insofar as we discriminate and understand the eternal relations of finite and infinite.

This is our fate, to know and to receive only what we are, yet to increase in the higher strength and wisdom to the degree that we consciously and freely choose it to the exclusion of all else, since wisdom is never forced upon us, but ever awaits our free and unqualified acceptance. Here, more truly than in any other sphere of human thought, everything depends upon the will or desire.

It is the one who has lived and suffered, conquered, thought, and practiced his own truest wisdom, who moves with fate. He is no longer as one among thousands, but himself a mover, a sharer of power, cooperating in intelligent companionship with the Father. Then dawns the Christ-consciousness, with its accompanying life of self-sacrifice; and the faithful soul enjoys a personal relationship with God whom he now knows through actual experience to be literally the All.

We can conquer anything that lies between us and our destiny. It would be strange indeed, if, granting that an infinitely intelligent Spirit sent us here for some purpose, this were not so. It would be strange, too, if any experience in the individual career were without its meaning in the divine economy. If, then, we can assume this, too; if, in place of the cruel fate which, as we thought, cheated us out of our just dues and defeated our hopes, there is a larger Fate that somehow needed for us just what we passed through, there is no room for regret, no cause for complaint, since in regretting and complaining we are finding fault with Omni-science itself. It is not for us to say that life is not worth living. Our life, such as it is, belongs to a grander Life, to which we must ever turn in order to see the meaning of our own. And experience becomes infinitely pleasanter the moment we realize the futility of all regret, complaint, and opposition.

Happiness

It is well to observe what a range of thought and sentiment is opened up by genuine happiness, and then, when the spirit of depression weighs heavily upon us, to recall these conditions, to let the morbid thought languish for mere want of attention, to stir one's self, to arouse a forced happiness if one cannot shake off the heavy spirit in any other way.

It is a matter of economy to be happy, to view life and all its conditions from the brightest angle. It enables one to seize life at its best. It expands the soul. It calls power to do our bidding. It renews. It awakens. It is a far truer form of sympathy than that mistaken sense of communion with grief and suffering which holds our friends in misery instead of helping them out of it. It is a far nobler religion than that creed which Causes one to put on a long face, and look as serious as possible. Once more, there is something wrong in our philosophy if it sanctions melancholy and pessimistic thoughts. We have not yet looked deep enough into life. We have never got beyond being impressed by the sadder and gloomier side of life. We are still thinking and acting contrary to, not in harmony with, the happy world of nature by which we are surrounded. By maintaining this mournful attitude, we show our want of faith in the goodness of things as much as when we fear. A deep, unquenchable spirit of joy is at once the truest evidence that we believe in the beneficence of the Father, and that we have penetrated deep enough into life's mystery to see how best, most economically, most courageously and helpfully to take it.

Beauty

The world within and without our consciousness may be, and probably is, perfectly beautiful, even to the minutest detail. But since beauty, like our perception of the world at large, consists of external arrangement, and inward emotion dependent on our organism, it does not exist for us until we see it in right relations, until the aesthetic sense has been quickened through the contemplation of beautiful ideas. More beauty environs us than we can discover in a lifetime; and in the history of the individual, as in the development of the race, the perception of beauty increases with the expansion of the intellect, so that the characterless landscape of youth may become a vision of charming lights and shades to the matured artist.

Behind, beyond, beneath all that passes is an eternal totality or whole of being, which always was and always will be what it now is, which always was and always will be everywhere. Its character, its wisdom and will, make it the living All or Absolute, whence springs the wonderful diversity of the world. All that exists lives with it. All that exists is beautiful, needed, and good, as parts of the Perfect Whole. We catch but glimpses of its glory as it passes from its own purity of perfection down through all the orders and struggles of life, and hence upward to self-recognition in man; but always it is there, ever here, and unchanging in essence. It is the highest joy of the finite to witness its revelations in the great world of nature and in the realm of spiritual consciousness within.

Chapter Five

Silence

It is in these moments of calm decision, when we realize our relationship to eternal power, that the mind changes and brings all things round to correspond to our deep desire. The ideal of daily conduct is to maintain this inward repose, to keep it steadily and persistently in view, to regain it when we lose it, to seek it when we need help, to have a calm center within which is never disturbed, come what may, — a never-yielding citadel of the higher Self.

To know how to rest, this is the great need of our hurrying age. We are too intense, too active. We have not yet learned the power and supremacy of the Spirit nor the value of quiet, systematic thinking. We struggle after ideas. We read this book and that, and go about from place to place in search of the latest and most popular lecturer instead of pausing to make our own the few great but profoundly simple laws and truths of the Spirit. We are unaware of the power and value of a few moments of silence. Yet it is in our periods of receptivity that we grow. Not while we actively pursue our ideas do we get the greatest light. Oftentimes, if the way be dark and we can get no help, it is better to cease all striving, and let the thoughts come as they may, let the Power have us; for there is a divine tendency in events, a tendency in our lives which we can fall back on, which will guide us better than we know, if we listen, laying aside all intensity of thought, and letting the activities settle down to a quieter basis.

Silence invites the greatest power in the world, the one Power, the one Life. Let us be still in the truest and deepest sense of the word, and feel that Power. It is the All in all. It knows no space. It knows no time. Its slightest activity is universal and eternal. It surrounds us here and now, in this present life, this beautiful world of nature, of law and order, this inner world of thought and the soul. It is the supreme wisdom and perfect love. It knows no opposition. There is naught to disturb its harmonious, measured, and peaceful activity. It is beauty and peace itself. Its love and peace are present here with us. Let us then be still. Peace, peace, there is nothing to fear. In this one restful happy moment we have won the peace of eternity, and it is ours forever.

If we habitually realize what it means to dwell with God, what the soul is, and how it is approaching completion, and keep the ideal of adjustment to life ever before us, pausing in silent receptivity whenever we become too intense, into the thought will steal the renewing and strengthening Power, which will prepare us for the day of sorrow and the hour of supreme suffering.

The adjustment, the poise, the experience of silence, is a realization. The moment comes when the individual has nothing to say: the power of conscious thought becomes subordinated to a higher power, the Spirit. One cannot speak. One can only observe in silent wonder, in awe at the presence of such power, which the individual feels incompetent to control. This, in a word, is the highest healing, the most effective, the least personal, and the hardest to describe. One can only say: Here is the Life, the Love, the Spirit. I have dwelt with it for a season. Go thou to the fountain-head. It will speak to you, and be its own evidence.

Healing

Again, the striving of certain sensations to make themselves consciously perceived and admitted by us characterizes all our joys and our sorrows, all our aches and pains; and it often rests with us whether to recognize and thereby increase the intensity of our emotions or to turn the will elsewhere. The body is striving to keep itself in repair, each one of its parts is striving to maintain its due place in the physical economy; and this tendency to regain equilibrium is so well known to us that we rely upon it to restore all injuries. In fact, we have never discovered the limit of its healing power.

Rightly understood, pain is the conflict of two elements, a higher and purer element coming in contact with a lower, and trying to restore equilibrium. It is remedial. It is beneficent, the most beneficent of all nature's arrangements, the best evidence of the unceasing devotion and presence with us in every minutest detail of life of a resident restorative power. Through it we are made aware that we have a life not wholly our own that cares for us, and is capable, perfectly competent, to take us through any possible trouble, since it is there only for our own good, since it is itself thoroughly good.

When we learn that it is a matter of economy never to rehearse the symptoms of disease, never to get angry, never to cherish ill-will, revengeful or unforgiving thoughts, never to make enemies, but always to be charitable and friendly, kind, good-natured, and hopeful, we shall not need to be told how we caused our own disease; nor shall we need to say, "I will not think these wrong thoughts any more," for they will die out of themselves.

The discovery is made that, by maintaining a quiet, trustful, reposeful state of mind, inspired by genuine understanding of the process that is actually going on, the whole being is kept open, permitting the natural activities to operate unimpeded and without suffering. Here is the turning-point away from matter, mental pictures of suffering and theories of disease into spirit and the stronger, purer, higher life, where one never speaks of one's self as diseased, but where the same Power which once made itself known through suffering, because one opposed it, now causes good health, because one moves with it. Here is the way of escape from the narrowing thought of life in the present, in time, into a hopeful realization of what one's experience means as a part of eternity; and, when one contemplates the end, the outcome, one is no longer entangled in consciousness of the means, the process.

The first point to note is that one cannot judge by physical sensation, but should look beyond it In sensitive natures the sensation of pain is very much exaggerated and is no guide at all. Sometimes the sensation is so keen and the pressure reduced to such a fine point that one's consciousness is like a caged bird fluttering about in vain endeavor to escape. Shut in there with such intense activity, the wildest fears are aroused when there is no real cause for alarm. The trouble is simply very much restricted. The Power is pressing through a very narrow channel; and relief will come in due time if one be quiet, patient, not trying to endure the pain, but letting the Power complete its task.

It is a truism to-day to affirm that miracles are impossible. The whole fabric of nineteenth-century science rests on the knowledge that law is universal If, then, such cures occur, — and they are too widely attested to doubt them, — they must take place in accordance with a certain principle. This principle is evidently the one already suggested; namely, that the bodily condition changes when the emotions are touched, — not only in sudden cures, but in all that constitutes the emotional life. And the reason is found in the existence of the subtle intermediary known as spiritual matter, which immediately responds to the slightest change of feeling, and translates it into the bodily condition.

The stronger the emotion, other things being equal, the more remarkable the effect or cure. Emotion of a certain sort — noticeably, expectant attention accompanied by implicit faith on the part of an invalid before a sacred relic — has a wonderfully expansive and liberating effect on the body. The whole thought is concentrated on what is about to occur; the individual is lifted above self by the emotional experience; and the physical forces are no longer hampered by fear, morbid awareness of sensation, and the thousand and one feelings which interfere with the natural restorative power of the body. The emotion frees, opens the body, so that the interpenetrating forces may once more circulate between the particles. Density is broken up. An expansion takes place; and a process of change which usually occupies many weeks or months is completed in a short time, resulting in the cure of many so-called incurable diseases.

Of all known forms of the one energy, then, thought is the most powerful, the most subtle, and, probably, the least understood. Used ignorantly, it brings us all our misery; used wisely, its power of developing health and happiness is limitless. It is essential to a just understanding of it, and to the knowledge of how to help one's self, that the reader bear in mind the central thought of each of the foregoing chapters. For we have learned that all power acts through something; and, in order to understand how the realization of the Spirit can break up an organic or chronic physical disease, so called, one must remember how such a disease is built up and what the power behind thought really is.

It is the thought, the mental attitude, the direction of mind which governs the whole process. Before the sudden cure can result, there must be faith, expectant attention; and, if the person have implicit faith, the whole individual is governed by this one powerful direction of mind. The emotional experience unconsciously opens the soul to the Life or Spirit, which, like heat, enters into and expands the whole being, just as the warm sunlight penetrates the very fiber of the plant. It is the Spirit that performs the cure, not the personal thought or faith. The human part consists in becoming receptive, in withdrawing the consciousness from self and physical sensation and becoming absorbed in the expected cure.

Simply to discover that so much depends on our mental attitude is of itself sufficient knowledge to work a wonderful change in the lives of those who ever bear this vital truth in mind; for, if we begin life afresh, with a determination to see only the good, the real meaning and spirit of things, it will be impossible for our old habits of thought, our fears, and inherited notions about disease, to win their way into consciousness. The road to better health, to unhoped-for happiness and freedom, is open before us. The better health shall be ours if we have the will, for nothing can resist the power of thought. The body, our fixed directions of mind, and even our temperaments will yield when we learn how to use this marvelous power.

In considering the qualities and composition of matter, we learn that the phenomenon of expansion and contraction is one of its most noticeable characteristics. Turning to the mental world, we find the same principle repeated; namely, that thoughts are harmful or healthful to the degree that they expand and contract the inner being. Fear, jealousy, anger, and all selfish or belittling emotions have a tendency to draw one into self, to shut in and restrict the. activities, impeding the natural life and restorative power of the body, and developing a condition from which, if it be long maintained, nature can only free us by a violent reaction: whereas a pleasurable emotion, such as one feels when listening to a familiar melody or the strains of a great symphony, causes the whole individual to expand and sends a thrill to the utmost extremities of the being.

The mere effort to become inwardly still is sufficient to awaken this sense of power, as though one were for the moment a magnetic center toward which radiate streams of energy. And, if the reader has sought this silence in order to get relief from pain or some other uncomfortable sensation, there is doubtless a consciousness of pressure or activity in some part of the being, as though the resident power were trying to restore equilibrium. To unite in thought with this quickening power is, in general terms, the first step in the process of self-help by the silent method.

For, through this experience of receptivity — it is an experience rather than a process of thought — one becomes connected with a boundless reservoir of life and healing power. The healing process is, in fact, one form of receiving life. We do not originate life. We use it, we are animated by it; for it already exists. Our individual life is a sharing of universal life. We possess it by living it; and. to partake of it is the commonest yet the highest privilege of man.

In due time, if this realization be repeated until one learns how to be still and receptive, one will surely become conscious of benefit and a quickening of the whole being. The mere form of words is nothing; for, once more, it is the Spirit which is the essential, the power behind the words, the experience which all must have in order to know its depth and value.

The process of silent help is, in fact, one of adjustment to the actual situation in the moment of trouble, — the realization that, individually, one has little power, even of the will, as compared with this higher Will, but that all that is demanded of the individual will is co-operation. God seems to need us as much as we need him. He asks thoughtful receptivity, and readiness to move with the deepest trend of the individual life.

This is one of the quickest and most effective means of self-help, — this settling down, down, calmly and quietly, into one's deeper and larger self, into present usefulness and equanimity, where reside the greatest strength and the greatest power.

What a change would come to sick and suffering humanity if all physicians would adopt this helpful method, and cease all this disease-creating talk about symptoms, — if people would throw off all slavery to medical opinion ! The best doctors would still have plenty to do, and there would still bis need of the skilful surgeon. The world's suffering would be infinitely less, and we should then have an army of men striving to teach all-round self-development and good health.

The mother's love, the friend's devotion, is thus the means of keeping many a soul in this present life when all other means have failed, — failed because they could not touch the soul, — whereas the communion of soul with soul through the truest affection opens the door to that higher Love which thus finds a willing object of its unfailing devotion.

It is humility, willingness to learn, which opens one to the All-knowledge within; and, if one approach this experience in a purely intellectual attitude, one is not likely to feel the warmth of the Spirit, since everything depends on the receptivityor direction of mind.

Mastery

Not all at once can the soul master its objective passions, and be truly ethical in its outer life. True wisdom consists in careful adjustment of means to ends, in slow, patient, persistent overcoming in close imitation of natural evolution, not in assuming that the victory is already won. It is a serious mistake to make this assumption. The entire life must be regenerated; and this is the work of time, for otherwise it is not healthy. He is truly aware of the higher law who at last really begins to practice what he preaches, when he at last obeys the law, and ceases
once for all to be a hypocrite. This it is to be a man: to be and not seem, to do and not simply to talk, to have the right ideal, the true motive, and patiently to
transform conduct in accordance with it.

To become conscious of a weakness is to have won half the victory. To become conscious of the process, and yet to live above it, is to avoid the friction which ignorance once caused us. It is sublime trust that we need. If one has made a change for the better in one's conduct, and traced it back to some new determination fixed in the sub-conscious mind during a calm moment of self-consciousness, is there any better method than to make full use of this most efficient process? Nature is surely ready to do her part: it is ours to sow the seed.

Anything which subordinates the soul, and prevents man from taking all that belongs to him as a free spirit in a beneficent world, any mistaken sense of humility or self-suppression, has a harmful effect on the whole life, and is evidently as far from a normal attitude as strong self-conceit. If one have continued impulses to do good, and suppress them, a reaction is sure to follow. It is better to express the impulse, even in a slight way, if one cannot realize one's deepest and fullest desire. Theological creeds often suppress the soul. One feels a desire to be larger, freer, and to think for one's self. Want of charity, continued fault-finding, the attempt to do a task that is beneath one, narrows the soul. Love, of the truer sort, broad thinking, open-heartedness, happiness, expands it, and has a marked effect on the health. Sacrifice of individuality to the control of a stronger mind suppresses the soul. Education often crushes out originality.

Those who reach out after the ideal as though it were somewhere afar off and not immanent in the real, who look forward to the future with a nervous strain instead of living in the present, where help is alone to be found, lose what little poise they have, and fly aloft on a burst of enthusiasm. The consciousness is concentrated wherever we send our thought; and, if we reach out or pray to God as a distant being, the thought is sent away from its proper sphere. It were better not to have ideals at all than to strain after them, and assert that they shall become facts at once; for nature's method of measured transformation through evolution is the only wise and health-giving course to pursue.

Those who are nervously inclined will find it necessary to stop themselves many times a day when they discover that they are under too great pressure. They will find themselves hurrying unnecessarily or inwardly excited. Oftentimes all that is needed in order to prevent serious mental and physical trouble is to take off this pressure, and find this quiet inward center. It is wonderfully refreshing and removes fatigue to relieve the pressure and open the spirit to the healing power. Simply to turn away from self, and all that destroys repose, to the Self which knows nothing but peace, is sufficient to give one help and strength at any time and in any place. The wise direction of mind opens the door to help. If we trust, if we expect it, the help will come, whereas the effort to make it come will put an obstacle in its pathway.

There is an easiest, simplest way of doing everything, with the least degree of strain and nervous anxiety. We do not learn it while we hold ourselves with the grip of will-power, when we try to work our brains, and force the activities into a given channel. "Self-possession forgets all about the body when it is using it." It interposes no obstacle to the physical and mental forces. It discovers the easiest method of concentration through inward repose, and finds in this quiet restfulness the greatest protection from nervous reaction and fear.

If we dwell in eternity, why need we hurry in soul, whatever bodily hurry may be required? Why should we not dwell here in the everlasting now, instead of reaching off somewhere in thought, anticipating the future and death, as though there would ever be a break in the stream of life? If we, as souls, dwell in eternity, is not our life continuous? It surely cannot die if it enlarges into the infinite, eternal life, else it would not be life, but mere physical change.

Revelation

All so-called revelation is commensurate with the character of its recipient It is never infallible. It is therefore "far nobler to comprehend than merely to perceive." Not he who merely thinks or reasons about life, not he who is occasionally illumined, but he who both lives and reasons, patiently comparing vision with vision and philosophy with philosophy, thereby discovering why all Systems are inadequate, yet partly true, — only that man who persistently asks himself what and why he believes, and what his visions mean, is in possession of trustworthy wisdom or truth.

The Whole

Since this ineffable Whole of beauty, wisdom, and power is literally the All, there could be no other independent being or reality; for all that exists has its being in that Ultimate, beyond which thought can never go. No part is real, self-sufficient, or good in itself, or completely self-knowing. Man cannot know himself as he really is, cannot understand the world, a friend, life, until all this has found its eternal setting in the background of the truly real. No thought, no emotion, no longing, no prayer, falls outside the all-inclusive thought, the eternity of love and wisdom toward which we aspire.

Who can tell the meaning of events in this unfinished stage of society, where the majority of people are still selfish and unreasoning? Who shall say that in the light of the whole, which alone gives reality, there is not some rich compensation for all that is heart-rending and sinful? Who shall say that the divine experience is not the richer and the more beautiful just because of this infinite variety of finite life with all its sins and its shortcomings? Are you willing to condemn the world on the basis of your scant wisdom before you learn the meaning of life in its ultimate sense?

We learn of the existence of ourselves through the discovery that other beings exist, and we only know of the existence of the outer world in its relation to or contrast with our own finite consciousness. On the other hand, these opposed relationships could not exist unless there were an ultimate reality, or Being, persisting through all these changes of substance and force. Spirit, the Self, God, is undeniably one. Only the Whole is self-consistent, only the All is absolutely real, — permanent in all its manifestations and complete through all its parts and through us.

Plotinus, the father of Western mysticism, says, "The mind that wishes to behold God must itself become God." Self-consciousness must be transcended, reason silenced, self-activity renounced, and all thought must give place to the mystical ecstasy; for thought is a desire to know, and in the ecstasy there is no desire. Mysticism has therefore been defined as "the belief that God may be known face to face, without anything intermediate." The most consistent mystics therefore unqualifiedly say, "I am God, you are God, all is God."

It is the high privilege of every human being to betray this spiritual Permanent, vivifying the pettiest details of our transient existence. Any thought, any occupation worthy of man, may be transfigured by this higher consciousness. Every experience will become beautiful when thus put in its eternal setting in the background of the Whole.

Thought, then, and human truth, error, belief, theory, all that constitutes our knowledge of the world, is an abstraction from the realm of' feeling. Feeling, intuition, mere being, is not intelligible alone: it must be thought about. On the other hand, thought is never complete in itself, though it be uttered by the profoundest philosopher in the world, because it is an abstraction from the sphere of primary experience, and needs to be completed by the living Whole. Thought and existence are in truth inseparable. Each must complete the other. Each supplements and is absorbed by the other. Only the absolute and exhaustive Unity is the real.

O eternal Father, life and substance of all the universe, power, light, wisdom, love, and goodness, from which we exist, in which we abide, drawing from thee all that we are, and offering to thee our scant words of praise, we raise our thoughts to thee in frank confession of our finitude, yet with unceasing love, ever-strengthening aspiration and longing for closer companionship with thee. Accept the poor attempts to embody in our halting speech the beauty of our life with thee. We feel thy spirit ever present, we gather evidences of thee wherever we turn in the great world around. Yet the glory vanishes when we would speak of thy transcendent presence. We can only trust that thou feelest our longing, our unspeakable joy in existence, and that, poor as our witness is, thou wilt accept it, manifesting thyself in the hearts and minds, in the lives and souls, of those to whom we would extend the hand of helpfulness and the word of hope.

www.ingramcontent.com/pod-product-compliance
Lightning Source LLC
Chambersburg PA
CBHW050912120626
46552CB00004B/1530